Spirit Calling!

Are You Listening?

By Eileen McCourt

Spirit Calling – Are You Listening?

By Eileen McCourt

Spirit Calling, Are You Listening by Eileen McCourt - was first published in Great Britain in paperback during January 2016.

The moral right of Eileen McCourt is to be identified as the author of this work and has been asserted by her in accordance with the Copyright, Designs and Patents Act of 1988.

All rights are reserved and no part of this book may be produced or utilized in any format, or by any means, electronic or mechanical, including photocopying, recording or by any information storage or retrieval system, without prior permission in writing from the publishers – Coast & Country/Ads2life. www.ads2life@btinternet.com

All rights reserved.

ISBN-13: 978-1523355785

Copyright © January 2016 Eileen McCourt

Contents

                                                  Page

About the Author i

Acknowledgements v

Reviews vii

Foreword ix

PART ONE: THE UNTOLD TRUTH!

Chpt. 1:   The First Great Untruth 1

Chpt. 2:   The Second Great Untruth 8

Chpt. 3:   The Third Great Untruth 13

PART TWO: SPIRIT CALLING!

Chpt. 4:   Spiritual Exile 28

Chpt. 5:   Living in-Ego 31

Chpt. 6:   Living in-Spirit: Welcome Home! 39

PART THREE: THE NATURE OF HEALING

Chpt. 7:   Nature's Healing Balm 45

Exercise: Healing Planet Earth 58

Page

Chpt. 8: Sleep on it! 59

Chpt. 9: Prayer and Meditation: Going Within! 65

Chpt. 10: Crystals 77

Exercise: Grounding with Crystals 81

Chpt. 11: My time in Cherokee Indian Land 82

Chpt. 12: Return to the Garden 89

EPILOGUE: Our ultimate destiny? ....,,,,. .. 97

About the Author

Eileen McCourt is a graduate of University College Dublin with a Master's degree in History. She is a retired professional school teacher of History and English.

A Reiki Grand Master, she practises and teaches the following to all levels:

- Traditional Tibetan Usui Reiki
- Rahanni Celestial Healing
- Magnified Healing of the God Most High of the Universe
- Fire Spirit Reiki (Christ Consciousness and Holy Spirit)
- Archangel Reiki
- Violet Flame Reiki
- Mother Mary Reiki
- Unicorn Reiki
- Pegasus Reiki
- Dolphin Reiki
- Elemental Reiki
- Dragon Crystal Reiki
- Golden Eagle Reiki (Native American)
- Lemurian Crystal Reiki
- Okuna Reiki (Atlantean and Lumerian)
- Goddess of Light Reiki
- Tera-Mai Reiki Seichem
- Psychic Surgery

Eileen is also a practitioner of Angelic Reiki; Golden Rainbow Ray Reiki; Golden Chalice Reiki.

She has qualified in Ireland, England and Spain; in England through the Lynda Bourne School of Enlightenment; in Spain through the Spanish Federation of Reiki with Alessandra Rossin, Bienestar, Santa Eulalia, Ibiza.

Eileen lives in Warrenpoint, County Down, Northern Ireland and has travelled extensively throughout the world.

This is Eileen's third book.

Her first book, 'Living the Magic: Connecting the Physical and Spiritual Worlds' , was published in December 2014.

Her second book, 'This Great Awakening: The part we all play in this time of our Lives' , was published in September 2015.

Her fourth book, 'Working with Spirit: A World of Healing', will be published alongside this book.

She is currently working on her first book for children, 'Young in Spirit: A child's first Spiritual book'.

Eileen has also recorded several meditation cds, accompanied by her brother, pianist Pat McCourt:

'Celestial Healing'

'Celestial Presence'

'Chakra Cleansing, Energising and Balancing'

'Ethereal Spirit'

'Open the Door to Archangel Michael'

'Healing with Archangel Raphael'

The list of outlets for books and cds, together with information on workshops and courses for both practitioners and teachers is on Eileen's website: www.celestialhealing8.co.uk

e-mail: mccourteileen@yahoo.co.uk

Wooden carving of Native American in Cherokee, North Carolina. Note the large tear on each cheek

Entrance to the Oconaluftee Cherokee Village in the Smoky Mountains National Park, North Carolina

ACKNOWLEDGEMENTS

I wish to express my sincere appreciation to the following, without whom this book would never have materialised:

My publishers, Don Hale OBE and Dr. Steve Green;

Declan Quigley, shamanic practioner and tutor, for his contribution to this book;

Margaret Hurdman, for her continued friendship, support and encouragement;

My family and friends, both here on the earth plane and those back again in Spirit, who continue to watch over me and guide me from the Higher Realms;

A special word of appreciation to my brother Pat, for his musical contribution to my cds. Your talent, Pat, is God-given and your 'Angel Fingers' have brought so much happiness and joy to so many people! May you continue to give pleasure through your amazing gift for many years to come!

Bronagh, Emma and Sarah at Mourne Office Supplies, Warrenpoint, for their work in keeping it all together for me! It is a joy to work with you!

All who have bought my books and cds; all who have attended my workshops and courses, and, I hope, through them, have found help and guidance in some way;

All those who have written reviews for me, having taken the time to read my work;

A special thank you to Patrick who so unceremoniously retired my faithful carrier pidgeon and dragged me, screaming, into the twenty first century! Now you have to keep me here, Patrick! Good luck with that!

A very special thank you to Petra, with whom I shared those wonderful and very special days in Cherokee territory in North Carolina, just a few short months ago. It is only with each passing day that I realise just what happened in those mountains, and why I was drawn to Cherokee in the first place. Yet another lesson for me to learn that we are being guided by a greater force, an all-seeing, all-knowing force, making sure we are always in the right place, at the right time. Everything is synchronised; there is no such thing as a coincidence. I got exactly what I needed at that particular time. It was a great joy to share that experience with you, Petra! Thank you for the fun and laughter! You truly are a spiral of Light, radiating outwards in all directions!

Most of all, thank you Spirit for all the Divine inspirations, gifts and blessings with which you continue to flood my life! I just hope I can give something in return through these books; that someone, somewhere, will find exactly what they need in order to continue on their Spiritual path back to a life of peace and harmony, to a life lived without fear, where the soul soars and flies freely, to express itself as it is meant to express itself, as a joyous manifestation of the beauty of Divine creativity!

I am truly grateful for all that Spirit sends my way!

Eileen McCourt, January 2016

REVIEWS

"Another beautiful book by author Eileen McCourt. It touches the core of your Spirit. Well worth a read!"

Francesca Brown, the Angel Whisperer and author of 'My Whispering Angels' and 'The Voices of Angels'.

"Again, another well written, honest book by this author. Easy to read, which will appeal to all ages and Spiritual beliefs."

Lynda Bourne, School of Enlightenment, West Midlands.

" 'SPIRIT CALLING' is a tour de force in our ever-expanding Spiritual cosmos. Eileen's third book yields a home-made style of intellect and writing which produces and administers to the reader a unique mix of Spiritual truth and validity."

Clare Bowman, Spiritual Historian.

viii

FOREWORD

What an abundant, nurturing and unique place is planet earth! At this present time, however, Mother Earth is in a very fragile, fragmented, decimated state. Our beloved planet needs healing; the universe needs healing; the entire cosmos needs healing. To try to claim otherwise would be a futile exercise, and would negate any credibility this book might carry.

There is a great universal truth we must all understand. And what exactly is this great universal truth that is so vital to our very existence? That great universal truth is expressed in the statement that our beliefs and our thoughts create our reality.

Thought is cause. Thought is the cause of everything, no matter what, being manifested. Thoughts are real; thoughts go out from us in the form of vibrations, and all vibrations manifest. Every great invention, every great creation of art, every idea coming to fruition, begins as a thought.

We have brought our world to the brink of disaster by our thoughts; by our beliefs. Our beliefs dictate our actions. If we want to heal ourselves and our planet, then we must first change our thoughts; we must change our beliefs.

What thoughts and beliefs must we change? The thoughts and beliefs that have brought us to this fragile state in which we now find ourselves! This fragile state which we ourselves have created. Mother Earth continues to give, give, give. We continue to take, take, take. We have exploited earth's natural resources; we have scarred the landscape; we have polluted the waters and rivers; we have contaminated the beauty and uniqueness of Nature, all in our greed and lust for more and more. Always more.

We have not yet, as a species, come to understand that we are guests here on this planet. Mother Earth has volunteered to allow various forms of life to evolve here, and we are only one of those forms out of the many and diverse kingdoms inhabiting planet earth. We are supposed to be sharing, not taking over, not subjecting other forms of life to cruelty and brutality. But for thousands of years, man has done just that! Man has seen himself as the superior race. As a result, many of the animal species have become invisible to us. They are still here, but on a higher frequency, safely out of harm's way. It has been their collective choice to not interact with us anymore. And what does that say about us as a species? Hardly anything complimentary!

And we have done all this not just with our actions and deeds. We have done all this with our thoughts. Mostly with our thoughts. Our thoughts of anger, hatred, desire for revenge, desire to get more and more, - all manifest in reality. It is not beyond belief, therefore, that our present climate changes and weather extremes have a lot to do with the toxic fumes we are sending out in the form of our thoughts.

And as a species, we have also not yet come to understand that everything is energy; inter-dimensional, multi-vibrational forms of energy. All forms of life abound all around us, in other dimensions, on multiple, other vibrational frequencies, constantly inter-acting, constantly passing through and beyond, above and below us. We are merely one of these multitudinous forms of life, at present embodied in a dense-energy, human body, for the duration of this life-time only. We are restricted with our limited human vision, denied access to these higher vibrational frequency forms of energy until we progress Spiritually high enough to gain access to these other higher levels.

Science has, to some extent, been misleading us. Science has been misleading us into believing that if our five physical senses are not registering something, then it does not exist. Scientists need to open their minds and grasp the fact that other dimensions do, in fact, exist; they need to grasp the meaning of the '*Vibrational Corridor*', the

x

'Cosmic Elevator' and accept that we are not the only form of life in existence and that life does indeed exist alongside us in multi-dimensional, multi-vibrational frequencies, unseen by us, but there all the same. And since 2012, becoming more and more accessible to us.

When we limit ourselves to just our five human, physical senses, then we are indeed truly limiting ourselves! We have thousands of thoughts daily. We constantly experience thoughts. We are thinking creatures. That is what we do! We think! Yet! Have you ever actually seen a thought? Have you ever actually heard a thought? Have you ever actually tasted or smelt a thought? Have you ever at any stage of your life felt a thought? But we all have them! Constantly!

Likewise, have you ever seen, heard or tasted an opinion? Yet we are constantly expressing our opinions. Ever seen an emotion? Ever heard an emotion? Ever tasted an emotion? Yet we, as humans, are constantly experiencing emotions. Ever touched happiness? Ever held sorrow in your hands? We laugh, we cry; we absorb, exude and emit all sorts of emotions constantly. And we would never deny any of this! We cannot deny that a lot of what we experience in this earthly form of embodied energy is beyond our five physical senses. And we have got to move out beyond those five physical senses, we have got to expand our awareness, we have got to expand our consciousness, we have got to realise and accept the help and support being constantly offered to us from the higher Spiritual realms. Therein lies the healing we all so desperately need; therein lies the truthful explanation and understanding of who we really are, where we have come from and why we are here.

If we can change our thoughts, our beliefs, we can change reality; we can change the world in which we live.

The beliefs that have brought us to our present, desperate state are merely three in number. But what destruction, what suffering, what chaos those three beliefs have brought us!

In Part One of this book, I explain exactly what these three meagre beliefs are. Just three! Just three misunderstandings that are causing all the trauma in our world today! Just three beliefs that have unleashed such terrible consequences for entire humanity! Just three beliefs we need to change! And in changing these three beliefs we will bring healing to ourselves, to planet earth and to the entire cosmos; we will restore all forms of life to a state of well-being and joy; and we will have Heaven on earth.

We must have the truth! We must understand that we cannot heal ourselves or our planet until we have the truth. The universal truth! Then, and only then, can we heal.

It is just so easy! It is just so obvious! Yet so many of us are still not getting it! So many of us have not yet grasped the truth; the truth which, when we do get it, will set us all free!

All is not lost. All is never lost in Spirit. We are are at a very low ebb. True! But out of something bad, something good always comes. Always! Equally true! No matter how bad a situation has become, it can always be healed.

Spirit is calling us; calling us back to our true selves. But the big question, the really big question is, are we listening?

We all have free will. Free will is inherently programmed into our essential human nature. And because we always have free will, we always have a choice.

We have a choice as to how we live our lives. We can choose either to live '*In-Spirit*', which means living an '*in-Spired*' life; or we can choose to live '*In-Ego*', which means '*Editing God Out*'.

Each choice we make entails consequences. If we choose to live 'in-Ego', we experience life in separation from our own inherent, natural state of being, our Divine Essence, which is our true nature. When we make such a choice, we personify and draw unto ourselves all the harrowing, all the limitations, all the difficulty-fraught entourage that ego drags in its wake. We make ourselves ill!

When we choose to live in-Spirit, we live an in-Spired life, in synchronicity with universal and Divine energy; a life full of joy, peace and tranquillity; at One with ourselves, at One with all other forms of life, and at One with *All That Is*.

The choices offered to us are very clear! We came from Spirit, and we will eventually return to Spirit. We are Spiritual beings having a physical, embodied experience. But our real nature is still Divine Essence. That is who we really are. That is who we always will be. So why would we choose to live anywhere else other than in-Spirit? Why would we choose to live our lives in the dark recesses of materialistic impermanence, uncertainty, difficulty, when we can choose to live in the Light and Love that is inherent in living in-Spirit?

And why are so many of us still making that less attractive choice? That less attractive, that harrowing state of being, that has reduced our planet earth to the decimated, fractured, fragmented, fragile world which we now inhabit, that world which now needs healing so much?

In Part Two of this book, I explain how we have become Spiritual exiles, but now, like all exiles, we yearn for home. We did not find that which we sought in the land of our free choice, Ego-Land. As a species, we lost our way, and we are now searching for the road home, the road back into the Light, the road that leads to healing and to a state of well-being and wholeness. We can end our own self-imposed Spiritual exile. Once we have answered the call of Spirit to come home, home to our true selves, home to our true inherent nature, we can live a life of bliss and happiness, in alignment with the higher dimensional forces that come together for us to manifest, easily, our needs and desires.

In Part Three, I explain where and how we can all find healing while here on this earth plane. Nature calls to us constantly. There are messages carried to us on the winds; wisdom in the mountains, forests and rocks; melody and harmony in the waters of the rivers and the oceans. Nature does not force, but gently guides us, into a peaceful harbour where we find calmness, tranquillity and healing.

I myself recently experienced healing while in the mountains of North Carolina, land of the Cherokee Indian. It was there that I experienced Native American drumming for the first time. I myself am not a Shamanic Practitioner, so I leave the explanation as to what happened me there to an expert in that field, Declan Quigley of Anam Nasca. In Chapter 12, Declan, a Shamanic Practitioner and Tutor explains the nature of shamanic drumming and healing, and what exactly it was that happened to me, as the drumming around me intensified, sending the candle flames dancing up towards the ceiling.

So yes, our world, our universe, our cosmos needs healing. And, of course, we need healing. A lot of healing! The good news is that we are constantly being offered help from other dimensions and Spiritual vibrational energies beyond our own, dense, energy field of planet earth. Worlds are opening, realities are shifting, energies are re-aligning, beyond our three-dimensional understanding.

And the other good news? The other good news is that we will not be allowed to destroy planet earth. There are twelve universes in the cosmos, eleven others besides the universe in which our planet exists. Earth is a priceless, glittering jewel, radiating out into time and space, occupying a strategic position along the '*Vibrational Highway*', attracting attention from many who are concerned for the raising of collective Spiritual consciousness. Planet earth is the solar plexus of our universe, and as such, absorbs the fear in the universe, transmuting it all through our energy systems. And yes, we are therefore being watched!

We are being watched, we are being monitored, in a friendly, loving, non-invasive way. Remember, what we do here on this earth dimension affects all other vibrational dimensions as well. Civilizations much more advanced than us, perhaps even millions of light years ahead of us, are involved in this too. These other-dimensional earth watchers will take control from a higher, vibrational force field, a force field as yet beyond our limited human understanding. They are intelligent beings who are concerned about the welfare of the earth; intelligent beings who are concerned about possible adverse chain reactions out into the universe and out into the entire cosmos, all starting from us.

This book, just like my other books, has been in-spired by Spirit. None of these books, none of these words are mine. I am simply the conduit, the tool through which Spirit is getting the message to you, the reader. Something, some greater force, some greater power than me, is feeding into my subconscious during my sleeping hours, and the result is the books and cds that have materialised, somehow, through me.

My first book, 'Living the Magic', was written and published in just three weeks; my second book, 'This Great Awakening', was written and published in just two weeks. And now, with this book, what is happening? Two books are being written at the same time! This book, 'Spirit Calling' and 'Working with Spirit', are actually manifesting side by side. More proof, if ever I needed more proof that I am not the writer of these books. I could not possibly write two books at the one time! Only Spirit could do that! I cannot force the thoughts or the ideas. All I have to do is go with the flow; I must go with the flow! How easy is that! Spirit does all the work! Living in-Spirit guarantees me an easy, worry-free passage, in the secure knowledge that the universe is looking after me, steering me, guiding me, to fulfil my life mission. And what is there to not like about that? And why would anyone choose to live in-Ego when living in-Spirit gives you all this? Why would anyone trade in a life of tranquillity and peace for a life of trouble and hassle? I am no genius, but even I can work that one out!

And yet again, I ask that you discard all limited thinking and read with an open mind and an open heart, allowing whatever parts of this book resonate most comfortably with you to bring you to a place of hope, comfort and greater awareness. We are all led to the truth, the truth for which we are ready at any given time in our Spiritual, evolutionary process. Spirit has guided you to this book, so I hope you will allow Spirit to bring you some of the help, support and healing we all need and we are all seeking, as we travel further on this, our own unique, individual journey through this life-time, back to remembering our Divine Source, back from our state of fragmented cold exile, to a state of wholeness, to a beautiful life lived in-Spirit.

I send you Love and Light!

Namaste!

Eileen McCourt

January 2016

PART ONE
THE UNTOLD TRUTH!

CHAPTER 1
THE FIRST GREAT UNTRUTH

Planet earth is going through a massive shift in consciousness, as we exit the *Age of Pisces* and come into the new *Age of Aquarius*. The Age of Pisces was the age of believing; hence the dominance of religions and religious teachings throughout the world, which we accepted as being the truth. The new Age of Aquarius is the age of knowing; we are now searching for the truth, the universal truth. Hence all the questionings; all the rejections of old institutions; all the individual searchings for knowledge and truth which will lead us into freedom.

With this knowledge, we expand our awareness, our Spiritual consciousness, moving our understanding to a higher level, respecting the Divinity within each person and within every form of life.

Our thoughts create our reality. Every thought we have is sent out on an energy vibration into the ether and is bound to manifest somewhere. The beliefs we hold, instilled into us from an early age, are mostly the result of parental and school teachings and religious and societal influencing. The good news is that we can change our beliefs. The other good news is that we can also change our thoughts. And the most wonderful news of all is that when we change our thoughts and beliefs, we can change our world. We can change reality. We can change our world for the better; for the better of all. It's as simple as that!

In order to change any of our beliefs, we must first of all come to a realisation that they are false. We need to grasp the truth, the universal truth, that lies beyond our limiting, five physical senses. It is gross ignorance on the part of humanity that has brought our planet earth to the brink of disaster.

There are three main beliefs, three seriously mistaken beliefs, which have brought our planet earth into the dire straits of our present day.

So, what are these three erroneous beliefs?

The first of these greatly mistaken beliefs is that we are *separate individuals,* each following our own separate path, pursuing our own individual desires, without regard to anyone else.

We are NOT separate from everyone else. We are NOT separate from all other forms of life. We are NOT separate from Source, from 'All That Is' Fact! There is no '*I*' or '*me*' or '*you*', there is only the collective '*we*'. We are all in this together; we are all part of the same chain of Divine, universal energy that runs through all things, supporting all things, manifesting all things. We are all connected. Fact! There is no separateness. Fact!

All of creation, in its entire totality, is connected. It is in this understanding of connectedness with '*All That Is*' that will enable us to reach a higher understanding of ourselves as consciousness and energy, constantly changing, but immortal, infinite, never-ending.

As above, so below. Our planet earth is part of a solar system which is part of a galaxy, which is part of our universe. But we are only one of twelve universes. All the planets in the entire Milky Way, in all the universes in the entire cosmos, with their diverse, inter-planetary forms of energy, are all connected with us here on planet earth. All our actions, deeds and thoughts affect each and every aspect of this vitally connected, exquisite tapestry of life. Fact! Indisputable! Irrefutable!

Spirit Calling - Are You Listening?

All the sky stuff, all the earth stuff, all forms of life, are all one big living mass of energy. And each and every aspect of this affects all the others. There is consciousness in everything, in all that exists on earth, in all that exists in the universe, in all that exists in the entire cosmos. All consciousness communicates constantly and continuously on electro-magnetic frequencies, throughout all vibrational dimensions. These frequencies connect and have a universal and cosmic unified investment in working together for the benefit and highest good of all.

The trouble and difficulty with earth, however, at this present time, is that humans believe they are separate from all this universally and cosmically combined energy. Our current belief that we are separate and individual is a barrier to us seeing, accepting and therefore accessing, the wholeness end entirety of existence. All we are doing is disempowering ourselves even further, cutting ourselves off from the very same source that we need for our own existence.

Our earthly bodies respond directly to whatever is happening anywhere in this entire, vast network of creation, as we sense it all through our cosmic umbilical cord.

We have highly sensitive, internal mechanisms which work in tandem with all that is happening in all other areas apart from planet earth. The weather systems, for example! The effect they have on our physical bodies! How often do we complain about feeling 'under the weather'? How well we can tell the rain is coming by the aches in our bones and joints! Many of our physical ailments are a direct result of the weather. Our respiratory rate, our blood pressure levels, our metabolic rate, our blood circulation, our heart beats, our fluid circulation,- all are affected by the weather patterns. And the firmaments affect even our mental state! Especially our mental state! The word 'lunar', is encapsulated in the word 'lunatic', the moon having a great pull on our minds, and of course, on the tides of the oceans. Humidity affects our health, as do temperatures, altitude, wind direction and wind strength. Whenever the earth's magnetic field is disturbed, there is always a correspondingly adverse re-action in human physiology and psychology.

Ancient and medieval peoples knew and understood the connection between what was happening on the earth plane and in the higher forces and dimensions in the rest of the cosmos.

In Shakespeare's plays, we see how Nature cries out in anger against evil perpetrated on earth. In "Lear", in true pathetic fallacy, we hear King Lear surrounded by the fierce storm elements, cry out to Nature for comfort and justice after he has been rejected and evicted by his two evil daughters: *"Blow winds, and crack your cheeks! rage! blow! / You cataracts and hurricanes"*. Nature, through the storm, is crying out against the evil and in defence of the abused.

Again in 'Macbeth', when King Duncan is murdered, the Natural Law has been violated, and Nature and the firmaments respond: *"The night has been unruly: where we lay,/ Our chimneys were blown down; and, as they say, / Lamentings heard i' the air, strange screams of death..........some say the earth/ Was feverous and did shake"*.

Animals have an even more highly sensitive, internal mechanised system within them than we humans. They can literally hear the heart-beat of Mother Earth. Animals can sense when an earthquake is about to happen and they know to move to higher ground when they sense a tsunami. They are also much more aware than we are of another energy entering a room. Farm animals gather in around the buildings when snow is due and the animals in the fields shelter around the hedges when rain is coming; and before the rain clears again, they are already back out in the middle of the field. And how well they can sense our feelings and moods! A horse, for example, knows if we feel nervous when approaching it, as does a dog or cat.

We too feel our link with all other facets of the entire connectiveness.

Spirit Calling - Are You Listening?

When we live in harmony with our surroundings, we enjoy a sense of calm and tranquillity. If, for example, we love the sea, then if we are living in a forested area away from the sea, our body will not be in harmony, we will not be in a healthy state; we will not resonate with, nor will we be in harmony with the synchronised forces that mould and form us; we will not be in a matching vibratory rate with the geographical area. Matching vibratory rates create harmony; mismatching vibratory rates create disharmony and a discontentment within the mind and spirit, creating a general restlessness, the cause of which is very often beyond our immediate understanding. Even the colours with which we choose to surround ourselves bring us contentment and tranquillity if they match the vibratory rate of our aura; disharmony if they do not. Everything has got to be in perfect alignment; all vibratory rates have got to match if we are to live in a healthy condition. Colour, scent and sound vibrations are especially poignant sign-posts for us as to the state of our health. We all have natural elements that best harmonise with each one of us and if we are to be happy in our life, we must acknowledge and honour our inner promptings to follow the vibratorary rates that best resonate with us.

So yes, we are indeed multi-dimensional beings in a multi-dimensional universe, inter-relating, inter-connected on every level. The more we evolve, the more we grow in awareness and Spiritual consciousness, the more we will realise, understand and accept that there is a greater connectedness in the universe, and in all things. The more unevolved a person is, the more Spiritually unaware, the more Spiritually closed, the more engrossed and entrapped a person is in the physical body and the five physical senses, the more that person will continue to perceive himself and everything in his life as isolated, individual and separate.

The Grand Design, the Grand Divine Plan for earth is indeed a grand one, a mind-boggling system; a microcosm of the macrocosm; a tiny miniature version of what is happening in vast worlds and galaxies stretching out into infinity. What is happening now on planet earth, with the earth's vibration being raised and adapting to a new, higher vibrational frequency, is also happening throughout the entire cosmos. There is a great settling down going on, as all forms of multi-dimensional consciousness re-arrange and shift into a new alignment in connection with the cosmic, over-view of life itself.

Unfortunately for humanity here on the earth dimension, we have been programmed to believe this world is a competitive, individualistic place, where only the fittest survive. We have been imprisoned in this individualistic mentality for aeons and aeons of time, where we have looked with envy, greed and resentment on anyone who has more than us, in the belief that if they get more, then I must be getting less. Believing in our own minds that we are individuals has made us into the egotistical, capricious, envious creatures we have become, instilling into us a compartmentalised view of the world in which we live. We put up barriers between ourselves and others; we build walls of protection around ourselves; we hide our true selves behind facades and masks. In this individualistic thinking frame, we fail to get to know our neighbours. What we fail to know becomes strange. And what becomes strange to us becomes fearful to us. We harbour negative thoughts of insecurity, suspicion and envy. The green-eyed monster! The product of our individualistic way of thinking! Our greatly mistaken way of thinking!

We are each other. We are the collective psyche. We are the collective human mind. If one gets more, we all get more; if one man hurts, we all hurt.

The poet William Blake, born in 1757, showed great power of vision in all his works. In his beautiful, evocative poem *'On Another's Sorrow'*, he wrote: *"Can I see another's woe/ And not be in sorrow too?"* And again, *"Can I see a falling tear/ And not feel my sorrow's share?"*

Spirit Calling - Are You Listening?

Likewise, the poet R. S.Thomas, born in 1913, expresses the same sense of empathy with the tramp: *"I sleep in my bed/ He sleeps in the old/ Dead leaves of a ditch/ My dreams are haunted/ Are his dreams rich?/ If I wake early/ he wakes cold"*.

Thomas' poetry has a universal appeal, reflecting, as it does, the human condition itself, and how we are all affected by each other's circumstances.

Chief Seattle, a prominent leader of the Duwamish Native Americans, in the State of Washington, who pursued a path of accommodation to white settlers, and after whom Seattle was named, wrote: *"Man did not weave the web of life, he is merely a strand in it. Whatever he does to the web, he does to himself."*

And again, *"All things share the same breath- the beast, the tree, the man. The air shares its spirit with all the life it supports.'"*

I am you and you are me. We are all One. If we can rid the world of the false notion that it is every man for himself and that we are all separate individuals, then there will be no envy, no resentment, no fear. If I see myself in you, how can I envy you? How can I resent you? How can I fear you? I cannot! What a release for all of us! To rid the world of fear, envy and greed! And we can do it! All we need to do is see ourselves as One; One with each other; One with all forms of life; One with Divine Source; One with *'All That Is'*. That's all we need do! Progress along the path of greater connectedness rather than the pseudo-science path of separation and individualism! Change our thinking from our current belief of individualism and accept the universal understanding of the great, unified web of cosmic consciousness!

Happy days! Heaven on earth!

CHAPTER 2

THE SECOND GREAT UNTRUTH!

The second mistaken belief that has resulted in such havoc for humanity is the erroneous belief that *we are all only this body.*

We are NOT only this body! We are NOT only the physical! We are NOT only what we see with our limited human vision!

We are more than our physical body. We are more than a heart, a liver, a brain. We are an immortal soul entrapped within our mortal, physical body.

To view humanity as being in the physical only, and to perceive the purpose of life as physical evolution only, is to miss out entirely on the meaning of who we really are, and the real purpose behind our physical, temporary embodiment and our temporary sojourn here on planet earth.

We are Spiritual beings, having a physical experience for this life-time only, in order to learn the lessons we have chosen to learn during this life-time, for our own Spiritual advancement from soul infancy to soul maturity. And this life-time is only a tiny miniscule part of our long, exciting, wondrous walk-about across eternity.

We are essentially and fundamentally God Essence. That is our inherent nature! And we need to waken up and realise and accept this! And when each and every one of us realises and accepts this in ourselves, we will then progress to accept this same Divine Essence in every other person and in every other form of life in the entire universe. And when we accept this, we will have Heaven on earth! And why? Simply because, when we come to recognise ourselves, everyone else and all other forms of life as Divine Essence, we will not judge, we will not criticise, we will not condemn, we will not hate, we will not fear! We will send out only unconditional love. And unconditional love is all there ever is. Unconditional love, and spreading that unconditional love is what life is all about!

When you sit at a pavement cafe watching passers-by, what do you see? Are you looking at the body? The face? The clothes? Or are you seeing something more? An energy, perhaps? An aura? That person you are watching is a spark of the Divine, a magnificent, wonderful, beautiful Spiritual being. That homeless man you pass on the street, that drug addict, that alcoholic, they are all sparks of the same Divine energy as we all are. God watches, God speaks to us from behind the eyes of the poor, the down-trodden, the homeless, the hungry. Beneath the physical body, behind the facade, behind the veneer, they are most probably very highly evolved souls who have chosen to play this particular role in the game of life this time around, in order to give the rest of us the opportunity to learn to be kind and charitable, and so further our Spiritual development.

We each carry within us Divine Essence. We each have a part to play in this incarnation; a part which will serve the highest good of ourselves and all humanity. We have each incarnated many times before, and we will re-incarnate many more times, each incarnation being only a miniscule part of all the roles we will play in our progress towards enlightenment, towards totality, towards completeness. We are here in earth school to learn lessons; lessons which will raise our own Spiritual consciousness and the Spiritual consciousness of all humanity. We serve two masters: our own Spiritual evolution and the collective Spiritual evolution of all humanity. As a species, we are, and always have been, moving towards a common destiny, - that of Total Enlightenment.

You, yourself, wrote the script for your own life. You, yourself, chose the lessons you wish to learn this time around. You, yourself, chose the time and the place, the lineage and the blood-line into which you would become embodied, into which you would be born, in order to provide the opportunities that would best serve your Spiritual development here on planet earth. Everything that happens you here, happens for a reason; every person you meet has a message for you; nothing happens by accident or by coincidence. All is synchronised in the dance of life, in the tapestry of life that you, yourself, wove before you came into this incarnation. There is no point in blaming God for all the ills that befall us as a species. God does not interfere in our life plan. God does not interfere in our free will. And yes, our lives are pre-destined! True! Pre-destined from before we ever arrived here! But by whom? By ourselves! Each one of us is the craftsman, the architect, the sculptor, the painter of our own landscape. We are in control of our own destiny! That's the reality!

Contrary to what science and medical science has been telling us, our human body is only the shell, the garment, the guise through which we experience this physical world.

There is a lot more to us than just our five physical senses.

The five physical senses being limited in perception as they are, mislead us into thinking that we are no more than our physical body, and that reality does not exist beyond that which we perceive with our five physical senses of vision, smell, taste, touch and hearing.

Science has taught us to limit our experiences to just these five cognitive, sensory mechanisms. Science has not taught us about our aura, our magnetic field surrounding us in an oval shape, acting as a barometer to our Spiritual and physical health. Science has not taught us about our chakra system, the spirals of spinning, magnetic energy fields, vortices of energy interacting with each other throughout our body, connecting us to Spiritual energy, intersecting all levels of our physical, spiritual, mental and emotional being.

Nor has science taught us about our immortal soul, that over-riding part of us that has always been in existence as some form of energy, and always will be in existence as some form of energy, for all eternity. When we come into this life, we do not need all of our entire soul, only a miniscule part to help us through this time around. The greater part of our soul remains in Spirit, and that is what we call our *'Higher Self'*. Our higher self knows everything there is to know, absolutely everything; it is full consciousness, full awareness, unlike our soul portion that accompanies us here, which has only limited knowledge. And why does our soul have only limited knowledge? Our soul has only limited knowledge for our own good! We are not meant to know everything! Otherwise, why would we be here trying to learn? How farcical would that be? Our learning process here entails finding the pieces of the jig-saw and putting them together; joining up the dots; surmounting the obstacles; finding the clues and working out the answers.

Each one of us, as well as every other form of life, every place, every situation, every experience, is a series of magnetic energy fields. We experience life as the interaction of these energy fields. Everything is energy, everything is consciousness, and all forms of energy have the ability to store and retain information within that consciousness. At this moment, as embodied human beings, our consciousness is tuned to the dense, vibrational energy of planet earth, our physical embodiment limiting us in our vision of all the other vibrational frequency levels that exist alongside us. But when we pass over, when we *'die'* to this physical world, we will enter the consciousness of totality, Spirit consciousness, Creator consciousness, and we will see the whole picture. Our consciousness will then be expanded, as we exit this temporary physical body and move on to the next phase of our Spiritual evolutionary process.

However, we do not have to wait until we pass over in order to experience this expansion of consciousness, this state of expanded awareness. We can access all these other levels of reality from where we are now. From where we are now, our mind can be tuned to many different wave lengths of understanding and knowledge. As a species, we lost all this ability when we exiled ourselves from Source, but now we are returning to our Divine connection; the veils between worlds are thinning and we have greater and easier access to other dimensions and other vibrational frequencies and energies. In Part Three of this book, you will find where and how you can access these other dimensions and vibrations, through meditation, sleep, Nature and crystals, to name but a few.

Recognising and accepting that you are of Divine Essence and merged with Divine Source is not any form of Spiritual arrogance. Accepting your Divine nature is simply recognising Divine Spirit within yourself, and your own magnificence and power as a result of accepting yourself as the Divine made manifest.

When you expand your awareness outside of your limiting five physical senses, you have the power to not only experience healing from other vibrational frequencies, but you also become the power yourself. You are the power; the power to heal yourself; the power to heal the world; the power to heal the entire cosmos.

So, as you go about your daily life, remember who and what you really are! Do not limit yourself within the confines of your physicality; your physical body is only one of many identities that your consciousness encompasses. You are Divine Essence, magnificent and amazing in all that being a part of Divine Nature entails. You have the answers within yourself to all the questions you could ever wish to ask; within your own higher self, that greater part of your soul which resides with Spirit and with which you re-connect in full in between life-times.

Shakespeare's Hamlet speaks of the beauty and capacity of man and

12

his ability to transcend the limitations of the physical: *"What a piece of work is man! How noble in reason! How infinite in faculty! In form and moving how express and admirable! In action how like an angel! In apprehension how like a god! The beauty of the world! The paragon of animals!"*

And you thought you were only this body!

CHAPTER 3

THE THIRD GREAT UNTRUTH

The third great untruth, the third great misunderstanding that has led humanity down a long and torturous road is the mistaken belief, the mistaken, misguided, false belief that *God punishes*; that God is to be feared; that God is a Deity on high, in male form, dictating our lives and meting out punishments to wayward, deviant, defiant humankind here on earth.

NO! God does NOT punish us! God does NOT dictate our lives to us or interfere in our lives in any way; God does NOT operate on fear! God does NOT demand anything from us; God does Not command us to do anything; And God is NOT an old man with a long beard sitting somewhere up beyond the clouds, assessing, judging, condemning, granting some requests whilst at the same time denying others, commanding us *'Do as I say, not as I do!'*

Our beliefs create and dictate our behaviours. Indisputable! Our belief that God punishes us for our sins creates a vast network, a vast web of fear in which we all get caught up, entangled, strangled. Yet fear is the most destructive force in the world today; it is fear that drives humanity constantly into war against his own kind; it is fear that controlling religions and lay institutions have used for centuries to exert power over the masses. It is fear that keeps us in bondage, that inhibits our soul from flying freely, as our soul is meant to fly and not shackled by chains; suffocated by the dictates of others professing arrogantly that their way is the only way.

We have surrendered and given over to others, our own free will, that unique facet with which we are endowed, that ability and that right to think for ourselves. We have hitched ourselves to various religions in the mistaken belief that someone outside of ourselves can keep us in God's good books; that someone outside of ourselves can show us how to get to God; that someone outside of ourselves has all the answers, and that they will save us if we follow their rules without question, obey their laws, embrace their teachings, act according to their dictates. We have handed over to others the responsibility that is ours and ours alone; the responsibility to maintain our Divine connection; the responsibility to evolve Spiritually and to raise the Spiritual consciousness of all humanity. And all because we have this idea in our heads of a frightening, punishing God! All we have done is trade in one fear for another; replace our fear of God with the fear that each and every controlling religion exerts over us! Yes! Fear is the one negative attribute that has brought us to the verge of destruction where we are today!

As a species, we are still in our infancy; all on our path towards achieving soul maturity, which means a realisation, an awareness of the nature of God and an awareness of our own nature. As immature beings, we have not yet developed enough Spiritually to realise what we are doing. That is not an excuse for our childish, immature behaviour. Our childish, infantile, immature behaviour is just exactly that! Childish, infantile and immature. But we are children and immature in our present stage of soul development, hence our behaviour. We are the youngsters in the whole of creation, with numerous civilisations millions of light years ahead of us. And in our childishness, in our lack of maturity, we have not been behaving responsibly.

Our understanding of who or what God is has been interpreted down through the centuries by those who took it upon themselves to see it as their mission to instill into us their own beliefs, mostly the duality of God being a loving, compassionate God, while at the same time being a punishing God, an angry God, a God whom we should fear; a God who orders us to forgive, but who Himself denies forgiveness to those condemned to hell for all eternity! A God who orders us to show compassion, but who himself fails to show compassion for millions of his children; a God who tells us not to seek revenge, but who himself proclaims *"Revenge is mine!"* A God who tells us not to judge, but who himself constantly sits in judgement upon all of us! What a contradiction! What a paradox! It just doesn't make sense!

Fear of God is not a criteria for either holiness, Spirituality, raised consciousness or raised awareness. Fear will neither induce nor further any of these. Fear only undermines any and every relationship, and it certainly undermines our relationship with God.

There are only two underlying emotions in the world: love and fear. Everything, absolutely everything is encompassed in either of these two. We do everything out of either love or out of fear. Love is the positive; fear the negative.

We have been led to accept that God loves us, yes, but if we disobey him, if we go against his rules, he will punish us. And punish many of us for all eternity! We will never be forgiven! And all this from a God who constantly commands us to forgive all those who offend against us!

Sorry, but this is not love. And it is certainly not God's love! This is manipulation; this is love with strings attached; lust for power and control masquerading under the guise of love.

Love, in all its many facets, is unconditional. That means there are NO strings attached; NO conditions imposed; NO stipulations decreed; NO control exerted over us. Love means compassion; understanding; nothing to forgive, because we have not transgressed in the first place. God is Love; Love is all there is; therefore God is all there ever is.

Unconditional love is the only kind of love there is and the only kind of love there can ever be. Unconditional love means accepting yourself and every other person as they are right now, and all that comes with them; all that they are; all that they have ever been; all that they have ever done. Unconditional love means total acceptance. TOTAL acceptance! That means no '*ifs*', no '*buts*'. It is as it is. Things are as they are.

God is Love; constant, eternal, infinite, everlasting. God is NOT a person with periodic, erratic mood swings or explosions of vile temper, venting his spleen, brimstone and fire on whomsoever of us has upset him, during which time we need to run for cover or hide until we judge it safe to resurface again.

Unconditional love is synonymous with God. And with unconditional love comes freedom. The two go together; you cannot have one without the other. Free will is what God has given us, and in free will, we have the right to choose, the right to express our Divine Essence as we so choose to express it; the right to decide for ourselves; the right to demonstrate our Divinity in whatever way we so wish. That is what manifests the great diversity that Creation really is!

BUT! With every right comes a responsibility! We live in a world of cause and effect. We live in a world where our actions bring about re-actions and create either a domino effect or a ripple effect. What has

Spirit Calling - Are You Listening?

brought our world to the sorry state it is in today is NOT God punishing us; it is NOT God interfering to save humanity from impending doom; it is NOT God intercepting to save us from ourselves, to rescue the experiment of creation gone wrong.

WE OURSELVES have created this reality with which we are now faced. WE OURSELVES have brought about the present situation where, in a world of plenty and abundance, millions and millions of people are starving; millions and millions of people still have no clean water; millions and millions of people are ridden with disease and ill health; five per cent of the world's people own and control ninety-five per cent of the world's wealth.

And how exactly have we allowed all this to come about?

We have allowed all this to come about because of our beliefs. Remember! It is our beliefs which dictate our actions! Our beliefs about the nature of life; the nature of humanity; the nature of God. Especially about the nature of God!

Let me illustrate this mistaken belief further; our mistaken belief in where and how God exists; our mistaken belief in how and where we find God:

A wealthy man who believed himself to be very holy and close to God invited God to dinner at his house. He reminded God that he had always lived a good life, giving alms to the poor, fighting with nobody, exacting revenge on nobody; just living his life in accordance with God's laws.

The date and time were arranged for God to arrive at this man's house for dinner. Great was the excitement; great was the expense; great was the effort put in by all the servants. This was God coming to dinner, and there was no stone left unturned to make this into the most sumptuous feast ever. A feast fit for a King! A feast fit for God!

17

The arranged time arrived. No sign of God. At exactly the appointed time, a hungry dog began sniffing around the grand gates, but was swiftly sent on its way by the expectant servants.

Still no sign of God.

Then a poor woman with several hungry children appeared in front of the house begging for food, or for some of what might be left after all the festivities were over. Again, she too was ushered unceremoniously on her way, with no food and no promise of any later food.

Still no sign of God.

Next there arrived a poor cripple, who suffered the same ignominious dismissal as the others, but with the extra threat of having the dogs turned on him.

Still no sign of God.

Later, much later, the wealthy man turned to God and asked him why he had not come to the dinner that had been prepared for him especially. God looked at the man in surprise and said to him: "But I did come. Exactly as I promised. I arrived three times and each time I was sent away without being admitted. How often was I supposed to knock before you let me in?"

Let's face it! Our beliefs about God and the nature of Divinity have not been working for us! We have obviously missed something! We have obviously misunderstood something!

It is time to re-think! It is time to realise that controlling religious teachings throughout history have been nothing more than a form of crowd control, and, as with any form of oppressive control, there comes the time when the shackles, the chains, the binding ropes will be cast off. How often through history has hatred, violence and suffering, been let loose upon the world in the name of religion, in the name of God? Countless times! Countless examples of forms and degrees of barbarity, excessiveness and fanaticism have been perpetrated in the name of religion, in the name of God, each faction claiming that their God is the only God.

How often, too, have religious teachings changed throughout the years? First, the world was flat; definitely flat. Then it suddenly changed to round; definitely round. First, the sun revolved around the earth; definitely. Then the world suddenly started to revolve around the sun; definitely! First there was re-incarnation; definitely. Then there was no re-incarnation; definitely! First there was Limbo, where the souls of innocent babes went because they had not been baptised; definitely! Now Limbo has disappeared. First there was hell, damnation for all eternity, complete with fire and horned devils; definitely! Now that has changed. Changed since 1999, when Pope Paul II declared that hell, as a physical place of eternal fire and brimstone does not exist. That was replaced by the decree that hell is simply a state of being that we experience while in this life-time; a state of being whereby we have cut God out of our lives; a state of being, devoid of the Spiritual Light.

It is time for us to realise the truth. It is time for us to adopt Spirituality rather than controlling religion. What is the difference?

Spirituality is a personal relationship with the Divine; a journey inwards towards our own Divine Origins; our own connection with our Divine Essence, like a coming home, a coming home to our own true self. Religion has been exposed right down through history as a controlling, dictated set of dogma, manufactured by those with a lust for power; male-dominated; intolerant; manipulative; judgemental; discriminatory; separatist. It just has NOT worked!

It is Spirituality that is going to lead us out of the depths where we are now; not any form of controlling religion.

And it is Spirituality that is rising to the fore at this present time, in the great Spiritual Awakening which we are all experiencing.

So who or what exactly is God? How do we find God? Where do we find God?

How can we fix our broken connection with God?

God is all-encompassing, unlimited, unfathomable. That means that everything, absolutely everything, through all time and space, throughout eternity, through all forms of life on all vibrational dimensions, is all incorporated in God Essence. We are all varying, diverse expressions of Divinity in all of its multi-multi-multi facetedness; in the wild, abandoned, free extravaganza of creation; createdness in all its unique singularity and in all its combineness, in all its togetherness, in all its jointness. We here on planet earth are simply one vibrational frequency, one vibrational frequency amongst millions and millions of vibrational frequencies; our earth merely a dot in the infinitesimal number of other planets and life-forms that permeate all of Creation.

And God is all of Creation. All of Creation is God. And we, as part of that all-encompassing Creation, all-encompassing God, are all inherently firmly rooted within the unlimited framework; an integral part of the painting, the tapestry, woven into the vast, unlimited, unending canvas; the art work, the expression of Divinity in all its diversity, in all its joyful expression, in all its abandoned, wild freedom, in all its glorious, pulsating, dynamic expressions through all forms of life and in all varieties of behaviours. All manifestations of life, no matter what, when, or where, are simply expressions demonstrating variations of the single God Essence, the single Divinity. God is everything; God essence is in everything; everything is God; everything is in God. God is everywhere; everywhere is God. God is everyone; God is in everyone and in all forms of life; everyone and all forms of life are in God.

Everything is energy. Everything is in a form of energy, vibrating at

Spirit Calling - Are You Listening?

different levels. Higher forms of vibrational energy are those forms of life that have progressed through the various stages of development of Spiritual consciousness, Spiritual awareness, to an understanding of God, of Divinity, of the nature of Divine Essence, of our own Divine origins and nature; and who now exist in the higher, vibrational dimensions, still working towards completedness, towards Spiritual and soul maturity.

And yes! God is energy. Pure consciousness. The highest, purest form of energy there is. That energy that encompasses absolutely everything that is, that ever was, and that ever will be. And it is through us that pure consciousness finds expression; it is through us that prime consciousness creates reality. Prime Consciousness and Supreme Intelligence created us in order to experience. Experience what? To experience life in all its many-faceted totality, its diversity, its individualities, its uniqueness. We are simply God energy finding expression, through everything we experience, everything we do, think, feel and say.

And God does NOT dictate our lives to us. We ourselves work out the blue-print for each of our embodiments here on planet earth. We ourselves decide what lessons we wish to learn this time around. We each write our own script for life; we each choose the cast, we decide what part each person plays in our script. We create the stage design, the setting, the back-drop against which our script will be played out. That is free will in operation! And then, and only then, do we ourselves arrive on stage, making our timed, grand entrance. Everything, absolutely everything that happens to us, every experience, negative and positive, every person we meet, has already been put in place by us, and not dictated to us by God. It is therefore totally futile to blame God for any disasters which befall us!

And there is no judgement from God on how we perform in this, our life stage-production. We assess our own progress; how well we

21

performed here; how less well we performed there; and then we have a choice as to whether or not we will return for another round to try and improve. And so we begin to draw up the next blue-print; create the next script, and when all the circumstances are right, when all the requisites are synchronised, we descend from that vibrational level, down the '*Vibrational Corridor*', to take our first cry, yet again, in the physical, more dense, vibrational world of planet earth. To give expression, once again, to Divine creativeness.

Let me explain all this further in the analogy of the wave.

Picture the vast ocean. It rolls, it swirls, it billows, it surfs, it ebbs, it flows, it thunders, it roars. Sometimes it moves gently, sometimes aggressively. It sustains life, but it also claims lives. It demands respect. These are all variations of the ocean expressing its nature, its multi-facetedness.

Now picture the wave. The ocean has not ordered, the ocean has not commanded the wave to appear. The circumstances which were conducive for the wave to form have now synchronised, and the wave has begun its life. The wave can peter out before fruition, or it can continue to build up to the crest, before exploding in a last triumphant celebration of its uniqueness, its magnificence, its creative expression. The ocean does not look with disgust or intolerance on those waves which do not reach fruition at that particular time. The ocean does not admonish the wave: "*You bad wave! You have failed! You get back down there again!*" The wave simply retires, retreats, relaxes again back into the wholeness, the totality that is the ocean, and waits for the next time when it will try again; when it will try again to express itself within the totality of the whole ocean. Eventually, it will begin its journey again; expressing itself as it so wishes, all the time being supported, held up by the vast ocean beneath it, getting its life-force from that ocean, getting its power from that ocean, getting its impetus from that ocean. The wave, when it materialises, is an individual form;

an individual form in the manifestation of a wave. If the wave could speak, it would say "*Look at me! I'm a wave!*". Then when it recedes back into the ocean again, it would say "*Look! I'm the ocean!*" The wave is expressing its individuality as well as its infinite connection to the ocean, its infinite inclusiveness in the ocean.

In just the same way as the vast ocean is the life force for the wave, so too, God is our life-force; God is the support mechanism; God is the energy force from which we emerge when the time is right. We are an expression of that God energy; a manifestation of that God energy, unending and unconditional; with free will to express ourselves as one of the multi-faceted forms of infinite creativity. We are infinite creation, infinite God Essence, supreme and unlimited intelligence, expressing and experiencing itself. So God is a verb, as well as a noun. And what is that verb that is God? That verb is simply the verb of creating and experiencing that creating. The God energy is experiencing life in all its multi-faceted forms through us. The ocean is the metaphorical God energy; the wave, the metaphorical individualism of creative expression, emerging from, and returning to, the Source of its being, time and time again.

God, the highest energy, pure consciousness, has endowed all of creation with the mechanisms to drive evolution forwards. And at the same time, we have been given free will to express our Divinity, to decide how we wish to use our Divine ability, and that means freedom to use our Divine power for good as well as for ill. The whole process of evolution just unfolds in a manifestation of the diversity of the highest energy, that energy which we call God.

So how do we explain all the evil in the world today?

It is not just today there is evil in the world. We today, do not have a monopoly on evil just for our time here in the present! Far from it! There has always been evil in the world. There has always been suffering, death and disasters.

To explain this, let me replace the word evil with the word polarity.

We are here to experience life in all its totality, all its good and in all its bad. We need to experience opposites in order to understand anything that happens to us. For example, day-light is understood by us only if we compare it to the darkness of the night. And that is why the world is round! To create day and night! To manifest another aspect of Divine creativity! We do not understand what it is to enjoy good health if we have not experienced the opposite, ill health, in some form. We do not understand happiness if we do not at some time experience sadness. We do not understand peace if we have not experienced war or some form of unrest and violence. There is polarity in absolutely everything, and it is part of our existence to experience that polarity in everything.

Remember! We are here to experience! To experience life in all its multi-facetedness, including all its polarities, all its varying aspects. And that is why we just need 'to be'. When we 'just be', when we stop striving, pushing, exerting, when we stop trying to force an outcome for ourselves, the outcome we think should come about, we allow ourselves to live in the moment and do exactly what we are meant to do. And what is that? What are we meant to do? We are meant to just be! Just enjoy the experience of living! Just enjoy the miraculous experience of being in a human body that is so amazing, so wonderful, so fantastic! Just allow God energy to find expression through us; in all the ways we express our own individuality, through doing all those things we love doing! God energy finds expression through us in music; creative arts; writing; poetry; fashion; hair styles; food and drink; gardening; sports; developments in medicine, science, technology and transport. Even the ways we find to support our local football team! The silly hats, the banners, the slogans! The way we apply a bandage or wrap up a parcel! The way we shape our hand

Spirit Calling - Are You Listening?

writing! These are all ways of humanity expressing Divine creativeness! Divine creativeness, God energy expressing itself through humanity!

It is our mistaken beliefs, and our consequential actions, right down through history about the nature of God and about what God looks like that have brought us to the edge of the abyss; to the frightening place so many of us now see this world to be; a world abandoned by God; a world bereft of any hope for a better future.

It is our beliefs, our greatly mistaken beliefs and NOT God that have brought us to this point in the history of humanity.

Our three mainly, wrong beliefs!

Our belief that we are separate individuals, each out for self in a rat race of a world, where only the fittest survive; our belief that we are only this body, that we are not Spiritual beings having a physical experience in this mortal body, that we are not part of the inclusiveness that is God, of the same Divine Essence; our belief that God is a punishing, all-controlling, frightening Deity on high, who demands total obedience and servitude from us, his children.

Now imagine a world where these three greatly mistaken beliefs are rectified, changed, abandoned; a world where our actions change as a result of these three greatly mistaken beliefs being abandoned, being changed, being rectified.

What sort of world would that be?

That would be a world where everyone would have enough to eat; where everyone would have clean water; where everyone would have a place to call home; where everyone would have access to education and health care. And why? Simply because if we could only see ourselves as all One, all united, and not separate individuals striving to

25

get more than our fair share, then, in seeing ourselves in each other and in all forms of life, and in seeing each other in ourselves, we would understand that the good of everyone, and not just the individual good, is served in a world of plenty; a universe which constantly, lovingly, provides all our needs and will continue to do so. There would be no greed, no avarice, no jealousy. IMAGINE!

That would be a world where, because we see ourselves as Spiritual beings, embodied yet again here on earth to learn lessons in order to evolve Spiritually, to evolve not just individually, but collectively,- that would be a world where we would see each other as Divine Essence and where we would have the utmost respect for self, for all others, and for all other forms of life. Hence, no-one would live in fear; there would be no violence; there would be no wars; there would be no killings, no murders. Everyone would be safe! IMAGINE!

That would be a world where because we understand the true nature of God, there would be no religious factions or religious fanatics claiming that their religion is the only true religion and the only way to get to God. There would be total acceptance of all Spiritual beliefs, total acceptance of all differences and varieties of life. There would be no fear. There would be no strife, no strain. There would be enjoyment in just being, enjoyment in all this world has to offer us, just experiencing life in the moment, seeing the beauty in ourselves, in all others, and in absolutely everything around us in Nature. We would be remembering our Spiritual nature, our Divine Essence, our Divine origins, allowing the codes deeply embedded in us to be re-awakened, to guide us back home to our true selves. IMAGINE!

The words of John Lennon's song immediately come to mind:

"Imagine there's no countries / It isn't hard to do / Nothing to kill or die for / And no religion too / Imagine all the people / Living life in peace / Imagine no possessions / I wonder if you can / No need for greed or hunger / A brotherhood

of man / Imagine all the people / Sharing all the world / You may say I'm a dreamer / But I'm not the only one / I hope someday you'll join me / And the world will be as one."

And we do NOT just have to IMAGINE it all!

We just need to change our beliefs; unveil the truths; accept those truths. Then we change our behaviour. And then? Then we have a world where everyone is happy, free, fulfilled and living in abundance.

The stakes are high! It's all to play for!

We can do it! Let's do it! Let's do it now!

Bring it on!

Eileen McCourt

PART TWO

SPIRIT CALLING!

CHAPTER 4

SPIRITUAL EXILE

What is Spiritual Exile?

Spiritual exile means living in-Ego, in the foreign territory of the human-based, lower vibrations, where we *Edit God Out*. Ours is not the usual exile. We self-exiled; we self-exiled to a lower, vibrational form of energy.

That is not where we belong! We are, first and foremost, Spiritual beings, with Divine Essence as our true nature. For us to be happy, for us to live a joyful, fulfilling life, we must live according to our own true nature. The state of being in-Ego is a false, artificial, illusionary state for our natural Divine Essence in which to dwell.

For many thousands of years there has been a mass exodus, a leaving, a parting from, a rejection of our own inherent Divine Essence.

We forgot that we are Spiritual beings, having a physical experience for this short life-time only. We forgot that the body is contained within the soul, and not the soul within the body.

We turned our backs on the freedom of life, in the knowledge that we are Divine Essence and opted instead for the chains, the cage, the drudgery of slavery to the ego.

We made a free choice. A free choice to live in the land of the ego.

28

Spirit Calling - Are You Listening?

Living in-Ego means we have divorced ourselves from our roots, from Source. And we must bear the consequences of our free choice.

Living in-Ego means we are living in exile. Spiritual exile. We left the land of our birth, the land of our roots, the land of our Source and settled in the foreign, alien territory of gross materialism, greed, envy, fear, selfishness and war; the land of the ego.

In exile, we forgot our roots, our Source. We adapted unhealthily to our artificial, illusionary surroundings; we neglected the permanent, the immortal, the Spiritual, in favour of the temporary, the physical, the illusionary.

Our exile was self-imposed. We were not evicted. We were not forced away from our Divine origins. We were not being punished or abandoned. We left because, yet again, we wanted more. Always more. Ego raised its ugly head and we allowed our five physical senses to dictate, to embody, to encompass the physical world for us.

We became nomads, wanderers, travellers, across a hostile, barren landscape. We cast ourselves adrift, rudderless, on a vast, heaving ocean. We became lost, separated from our Source, no longer even knowing for what it was that we searched.

And worst of all, we gave away our power. Our power as a spark of the Divine. We allowed other, false ego-driven powers to lead us. And the result? This warring, fractured, decimated world in which we now find ourselves.

Like all exiles, we long to return home. We yearn to see the father-land once more. We are beginning to realise that we can no longer continue to exist in this fragmented state. And we are realising that we need to return from this fragmented state to a state of wholeness. Our souls cry out for contact with our native roots, for sustenance and nourishment that can only come from our Mother-Father. We

29

need to return home. We have had enough of this land of exile, this land that promised so much and delivered so little. We have heard the call! The call of the universe! The call of our soul! The call of Spirit!

And many of us are now returning home, the prodigal sons; home to our true selves; home to our true nature. We are ending our self-imposed exile. We have begun the long journey back to from whence we came.

Our return journey is a journey to within ourselves, an inner road to our own Spiritual nature, to our own '*Higher Self*', to a reclaiming of our own power as Divine Essence.

That call back home, that call to within ourselves, comes to us all in Divine timing. Many are well into the journey home, and many more of us are coming close behind. All others will follow. No matter how long it takes, we will all return home. We will all return to where we truly belong.

All the signs are good. The future bodes well. And why? Simply because of the direction in which we are now travelling. We have made the u-turn; we are moving back towards the Light; we are moving back to living in-Spirit.

We are safe.

CHAPTER 5

LIVING IN-EGO

There is only one of two places in which we can live. We can live in either the '*conscious*' state of in-Spirit, which is our true self, our Spiritual self; or we can live in the '*unconscious*' state of in-Ego, which is our false self. This latter is a severely limiting idea about what we are and who we are. It defines us as a physical body only, living within the confines of physicality, narrowing our experiences to that revealed by the five physical senses, which is only a miniscule part of the total, vast range of perception available to us.

The ego makes itself known soon after the soul enters the physical body, and exerts its influence throughout our entire life-time.

So what is this ego? What does it mean to live in-Ego? What is it like living in-Ego?

Living in-Ego means living a life where we *Edit God Out*; where '*I*' and '*Me*' pre-dominate; where servitude to self and gratification of self results in enslavement to a false, temporary, transitory, illusionary concept. Living in-Ego means living in a state of non-alignment. Non-alignment with what? Non-alignment with the universal energy flow. And living in a state of non-alignment with the universal energy flow means struggling, being restless, unhappy, unsettled.

Ego is synonymous with the false self; the illusionary self; the superficial self, and like everything else false, illusionary and superficial, it promises much but fails in the delivery. It drags misery, unhappiness, emptiness in its wake. It brings enslavement along with it in its entourage; enslavement to false hope, false fulfillment, false, unrealistic expectations.

Ego identifies with form; with the outer manifestation of form in its various facets, which include physical forms, thought forms and emotional forms. When we identify completely with only physicality, thoughts and emotions, we are totally unaware of our Divine connection, our connection to Divine Source. When we are ego motivated, we are confined, entrapped in our five physical senses. We live a sort of stagnant existence, never realising who we are, why we are here, or what we are here to do. So ego, therefore, can be explained as a lack of awareness of the connectedness with all other life-forms; a lack of awareness of the connection of each and every one of us with the whole, with the '*All That Is*'. Literally, this means *Editing God Out*.

When we exist in such a state of separateness, where we *E*dit *G*od *O*ut, we serve only the false self. Neither a recommendable nor a reputable master!

When we serve only the false self, we neglect, we deny, we negate the collective human consciousness. We are seeing only the surface, only what our five physical senses allow us to experience. We are failing to see the connectedness, the support mechanisms under the surface that maintain the whole universal energy which encompasses the whole of life, in every form, in the vast infinity of what we call creation.

And ego is not just individual; ego is also collective. Collective in the ego of countries, nations, governments, religions and creeds. And in just the same way as ego serves the individual, it also serves the collective. In just the same as ego manifests for the inividual, so too it also manifests for the collective. What ego does for the individual, ego also does for the collective.

And the result?

The result is that when we transfer all this individual ego onto the collective world stage, we get this warring, fractured, decimated planet

Spirit Calling - Are You Listening?

we now inhabit, where ego is running rampant, where ego is in control instead of being controlled. When we allow ourselves to live in jealousy, hatred, fear, judgement, desire for revenge, then we weaken our ability to recognise and use our full potential. In such a scenario, ego dominates, thrives and flourishes.

The ego is the source of all human suffering. And why? Simply because ego, the vampire, is constantly sucking from humanity, rather than contributing to humanity.

The twentieth century has seen two world wars, atomic bombs, biological weapons. All of this is resulting from fear and greed for power; humanity working from the false self, the ego, rather than from the Spiritual self. It is only when we develop and expand our conscious awareness that we learn to control the false ego.

What drives, what motivates, what sustains ego?

Ego is driven, like everything else in life, by the desire, the urge, to preserve itself; to remain in existence; to save itself from annihilation; to save itself from being wiped out. If we choose to live in-Spirit, the only alternative to living in-Ego, then ego becomes redundant, obsolete, defunct. And that is the last thing ego wants for itself!

Ego is motivated by fear, greed and the desire for power and control.

So how come this ego thing has so much control over us? How come we have allowed it to dominate our lives?

We allow ego to take over our lives because it makes us feel better about ourselves. It makes us feel we are superior to others. And, ironically, even though it continues to only operate on a temporary basis, it still manages to sustain itself.

Ego sustains itself because it works so hard to sustain itself! It permeates every aspect of our lives. It oozes in everywhere. It lurks in all the corners. It disguises itself, unrecognisable, unidentifiable, under its many guises.

And ego sustains itself through our human ignorance. When we live in-Ego, we live in an unawakened state, in a world of unawareness, in a world of unconsciousness. Unaware of what? Unconscious of what? Unaware of the connectedness of all life. Unconscious of the fact that we are all One, all One in the vast universal energy that sustains us.

So what is the way out of our dilemma?

We need to disentangle ourselves, separate ourselves from ego!

And how do we disentangle ourselves, how do we separate ourselves from ego?

First, we need to remember who we really are! And then, in remembering who we really are, we re-align ourselves with our Spiritual self, our Divine Essence, which brings peace, harmony, balance and the synchronistic flow of universal Divine energy into our lives.

Unless we know and understand the basic mechanics behind the workings of the ego, we cannot recognise it, and when we fail to recognise it, ego will trick us into identifying with it time and again again. It takes us over, an imposter pretending to be our true nature, our true self.

And ego's main problem? Ego's main rival? Ego's main enemy?

Ego's main obstacle, ego's main competitor is silence. And why? Because if ego allowed us to have silence in our lives, it would lose contact with us altogether. Then it would be exit ego! Ego gone; gone for good! Redundant!

So ego operates a keep busy, busy, busy programme; a do, do, do programme; a go, go, go programme; a get, get, get programme.

Ego is that little voice inside of us, niggling away at us, gnawing away at us, urging us, forcing us to go, go, go; do, do, do; get, get, get. More, more, more!

Ego tells us we are only this body, and as this physical body we are firmly rooted in earthly things; material possessions; worldly goods; worldly pleasures.

Ego tells us we are judged by the material possessions we manage to accumulate; the more we have, the more successful we will be in the eyes of others; the more we will be admired and emulated. Ego tells us we need all this stuff we buy for self; self has to come first and foremost. The egoic mind identifies the person we are with the possessions we have. We lose our selves in our possessions. We become that huge house; we become that fabulous car; we become that expensive piece of exquisite jewellery. We are identified by others as the person with that huge house; that person with the fabulous car; that person with that exquisite jewellery. We have made it big! So having material possessions, ego tells us, gives us an identity. Yes! True! But a false identity! Material possessions rob us of our true identity; our true self! But ego triumphs yet again, and so we find ourselves in competition, in a battle, constantly preoccupied with achieving the most, the best, the biggest. No pressure there then!

And how well those in the advertising industry can play on all this! Their job is simply to convince us that we need this or that product in order to enhance our lives; to simply convince us that the purchase of this or that will add something to our sense of self, in our own eyes and in the eyes of others. And so we buy it. Ego wins again!

Ego tells us we are separate individuals, in a competitive world, where only the fittest survive.

And the result?

The result of this separatist, individualistic programming by ego is competitiveness, cut-throat, man-eat-dog competitiveness; competitiveness on a massively destructive scale, where there should be co-operation on a massively productive scale.

The workplace! Ego in its element! The epitome of egotism! The workplace has become a place where ego dominates. A soul-destroying, rather than a soul-enhancing place. A place where creativity is stifled rather than a place where the soul's creativity is encouraged, engendered, furthered. A place where natural talents and creativity are stifled, smothered, suffocated, instead of a place where they should be fostered, sponsored and guided to fruition. Before industrialisation, all in the name of so-called progress, individuals expressed themselves and their talents in creative masterpieces; coopers, iron-mongers, stone-masons and the like took pride, joy, satisfaction and fulfillment in their work. The creative soul flourished. And that is what we are meant to do! We are meant to create! We are meant to manifest the diverse creativity of the Divine. God Energy finds expression through us. That is why we are here! To give expression to the multi-facetedness of God's Creativity, and to experience that Creativity in all its diversity. And what exactly has industrial machinery added? Only a faster production line; more goods produced in less the time; more money! Well done ego! Consumerism's best friend!

The workplace has become a place where we are valued and assessed according to how productive we actually are in creating more money for our employers. And those of us who generate the more business and hence the more money, are those who will retain their job more easily. No pressure there either!

The workplace should contribute to the overall enhancement and good of the community. It should not alienate or separate an individual from his own nature. Let's face it! Operating a machine, working on a production line, for example, does not exactly stimulate the creative part of the soul. In fact, all that has happened is that the soul has been taken out of work completely. Consumerism and increasingly higher production target levels are stifling creativity. Entrepreneurship cannot be conducive to all round enhancement when it operates only at the expense, or to the detriment of everyone else. Machiavellian principles, where the good of the individual can be sacrificed for the good of the many has been allowed to dominate not only our political systems, but also our economic and industrial systems.

And all this has come about because of the ego! Because the ego tells us that we are just this physical body; we are measured by the amount of material possessions we can accumulate; by how much money we can make; by how big a business empire we can build for ourselves. If we want to be noticed, if we want to be admired, we must be successful; successful in making money and gathering material possessions. Definitely no pressure!

So what else does this ego thing do for us?

In what other ways does this ego show itself?

Ego shows itself when we rant and rage against what is actually happening at any particular time. Road rage; having to get the last word in an argument; trying our best to get the outcome we think we know is best for us in any given situation; criticising; back-biting; be-littling people; demanding thanks or praise; asserting our authority over others; dictating to others how they should live their lives or what they should do; making others out to be wrong and yourself right; all of these operate from us seeing ourselves as superior to others. Probably the most frequent way in which the individual ego asserts itself is seen in our dependency on form for happiness. We crave satisfaction, fulfillment and happiness through acquiring more possessions; through acquiring the perfect body, the envy of all others. Like a child with a new toy, the novelty soon wears off, and we need another new material possession. We put our trust for happiness in transient, temporary form. We expect to find satisfaction in more, bigger, better, best.

And then we wonder why relationships do not last!

Relationships do not last because we demand more and more from them in order to satisfy our self-gratification, in order to feed our ego. We see everyone else through what they have materially; how they can best serve us in meeting our personal needs; how they look; how they dress; how much money they have. It's all about 'me, my, mine'!

This ego will only disappear for good when we realise how limiting and evil it actually is. Ego is not our friend, but our enemy. Ego does not give, it takes. Ego promises everything, but delivers only very short-lived satisfaction and transient happiness. We only need to watch the daily television news programmes, read the daily newspapers to see the destruction, suffering and trauma ego inflicts upon the world.

The bad news is that the unprecedented violence that humans are inflicting on other human beings and on other life-forms is testament to how rampant ego is in our world today. Fear, greed and desire for power, are powerful destructive weapons and it is these which feed the individual and collective ego. Failure to recognise our connectedness to the whole; failure to recognise that we are much more than just a physical body; failure to recognise that the good of the individual is best served through the good of the whole have all led us to this present brink of destruction.

And the good news?

38

The good news is that once we recognise the ego for what it actually is, then we can become more aware of our thoughts and emotions that feed that ego. And then we can experience the shift from ego thinking to awareness; to awareness of a greater connectedness to all forms of life; to a greater power than us; to an awareness of who we truly are, and when we increase this awareness, this consciousness, then we will be able to destroy the ego for good. And then we will experience the joy, the peace, the fulfillment for real; the peace, the joy, the fulfillment that ego promised us, but because of its very nature, could not deliver.

CHAPTER 6

LIVING IN-SPIRIT: WELCOME HOME!

Living in-Spirit is the antithesis to living in-Ego.

When we live in-Ego, we perceive only through the five physical human senses and we are affected by only what is encompassed in the world of this limited perception. Conversely, when we live in-Spirit, we perceive beyond the physical plane to an acceptance, an awareness of other vibrational energy levels with which we are directly and deeply connected.

Where living in-Ego is based on the beliefs of separateness, individualism, attack, condemnation, self-gratification, control, living in-Spirit on the other hand, is characterised by sharing, collectiveness, Oneness, unconditional love.

Living in-Ego is temporary, transient, vulnerable, open to attack on all sides. Living in-Spirit is unchanging, eternal, bullet-proof, non-vulnerable.

While living in-Ego sees the individual as the doer, the one who determines every outcome, living in-Spirit acknowledges that there is a far superior force than us, an infinite intelligence, a universe that knows our every need and responds to our every need.

Living in-Ego fails to realise that there is universal life energy flowing through all life-forms. Living in-Spirit accepts this universal life energy flow as central to all, inherent in everything.

When we are living in-Ego we feel we have got to be in control, taking matters into our own hands, to '*do*', to bring about a certain outcome. Living in Spirit just '*is*', letting everything just flow without any interference from the egoic self.

Living in-Ego is aggressive, competitive, struggling against the flow; living in-Spirit is passive, accepting, going with the flow.

Living in-Ego brings a sense of discontent, impermanence, always wanting more and uncertainty. Living in-Spirit brings deep contentment, joy, a strong sense of the infinity of life and existence.

Living in-Spirit allows us to be in touch with who we truly are; we align with all the other vibrational forces around us as we push the physical, materialistic self out of the way. And it is then, and only then, that we are able to tune into the abundant source of wealth, gifts and blessings that are being showered on us daily from the Heavenly and Celestial realms.

Living in-Spirit engenders our creativity. It opens our minds and

Spirit Calling - Are You Listening?

hearts, making us totally receptive to being in-Spired, where ideas flow freely as we are connected with Source in the great flow of universal, creative energy. And this is something that cannot be forced, demanded or commanded. Neither does it force, demand or command. It is here for everyone, we are all eligible to receive this source of in-Spiration from the vast universal energy source, but we must first be aware of it, and then we must make ourselves receptive to it.

Living in-Spirit is not a destination we aim to reach, but rather a direction in life that we take, a way of living that we adopt. When we are living in vibrational alignment, in-Spirit, we concentrate entirely on the good in the world. When we condemn or feel angry with evil doers, terrorists, those who inflict suffering in the world, then we have lost our focus.

Those who inflict suffering on others are the opposite side of the same coin to those who do good. We are all expressing the God creativity inherent in each of us. Those who inflict suffering have freely chosen to express their Divine creativity in that way. God does not make them evil or force them to become evil. Remember! God expresses creativity through all forms of life. And that includes us! We have our God-given, our God-bestowed gift of free will to act as we so choose, to express our creativity as we so choose. We can freely choose to move towards Spirit or move away from Spirit.

This world is a world of polarities, for reasons already explained in a previous chapter. Living in-Spirit means that we accept all the vast diversity of human behaviour and learn from it. We cannot judge or condemn because we do not know what anyone's life mission is; we are all here not just to learn lessons from others, but also to teach lessons to others; not just to receive love from others, but also to give love to others, unconditional love. We cannot fight violence with violence; we cannot destroy or wipe out evil with perpetrating the same actions. All we are doing in this case is making martyrs and enforcing the strength and survival of those evil ideas, those evil ideologies. To continue to live in-Spired on a daily basis, we must be able and willing to identify any of our ego-based thoughts that lead us into anger, judgement or condemnation, and then to replace those negative, egotistic thoughts with love, compassion and forgiveness, knowing in our own inherent in-Spired knowingness that only love, compassion and forgiveness can disarm violence and hatred. When we react differently, we are living in-Ego, seeing ourselves as superior to those with whom we are dealing.

Living an in-Spired life means that we understand and accept that we have created our own life plan before we came into this incarnation. When we understand and accept this, then we do not blame God or anyone else for what happens to us. We accept who we are and why we are here. We see only perfection in the unfolding of our plan, and we take responsibility for our thoughts, words and actions, knowing that the energy we send out attracts like energy to it. We recognise the occasions when we perhaps fall out of creative, vibrational alignment and we understand that in such circumstances we need to change our energy in order to bring ourselves back into alignment, back to living in-Spirit.

When we are living in-Spirit, we accept that we are not just this body. We know that our body is only the temporary vehicle for transporting our immortal soul through this life-time. And yes, of course we take care of our body; we nourish and sustain it. But, unlike living in-Ego, we accept our body as it is, not trying to re-shape it, to mould it into something it was never meant to be. When we live in-Spirit, we accept that when we have no further use for our body, we will discard it, like old clothing as our soul moves onto its next stage of Spiritual evolution. A sort of Spiritual re-cycling!

When we live in-Spirit, we live in greater awareness, greater consciousness, greater consciousness expansion. And when we experience expansion of our consciousness, we see the infinity of all creation, not just the tiny, miniscule part of creation that we experience when we live in-Ego. When in-Spirit, we accept the vastness of infinity, we accept the connectedness of all forms of life in the unlimited God energy. When we see the connectedness in all things, we see God energy in each and every form of life, here and elsewhere in all of creation. And when we see God in ourselves and in all others, then our very limited earthly vision changes; seeing the God energy in all forms of life negates any judgement, any criticism, any negativity. And the result? Heaven on earth!

Living in-Spirit manifests miracles for us on a full-time basis. We see all the magic in life; the magic in the material world around us; the magic of everything in Nature, all infused, all imbued, all in-Spired with the energy of Spirit, the energy of God; the magic in all the diverse forms of life here on planet earth; the magic in the workings of the human body, the human brain; the magic of all the interacting between all of us here on planet earth; the magic of all we experience through our five physical human senses.

But most of all, when we live in-Spirit, we experience from well beyond our five human, physical senses. Living in-Spirit means living in detachment from the physical world; living in the knowledge that the physical is only temporary, that the Spiritual is never-ending, on-going, infinite; that we are an intrinsic part of Spirit and as such, we are constantly being cared for, nourished and sustained in the vast network of creativity, held together in a never-failing support mechanism, an exquisite network of geometric designs, mathematical equations and light and sound vibrations. And in all of this, we do not need to struggle. We just need to go with the flow, in acceptance that all is as it should be; everything happens for a reason, beyond our human understanding, but for our own highest good; we are always in the right place at the right time, and we are all on our own Spiritual journey back to Source. Living in-Spirit means we live in acceptance of all this. And living in acceptance of all this enables us to see the wonder, to see the the magic in every moment of life, the synchronicities that manifest all that magic, and to step into and live our lives in that magic.

We all yearn for happiness, joy, love and peace. Our soul cries out for nourishment, for release from the addictive temporary satisfaction we get from adherence to the physical, from attachment to material possessions, from the struggle to be better than everyone else, to have more, more, more. We can find the joy, the peace, the love, the happiness for which we all yearn here on earth, here in this life-time. But we have to know where to find it!

We can find all this when we live in-Spirit, where we naturally belong!

Welcome home! Welcome back to an in-Spired life; welcome back to living in-Spirit!

Enjoy!

PART THREE

THE NATURE OF HEALING

CHAPTER 7

NATURE'S HEALING BALM

Nature! Earth's magical playground! Our escape mechanism from a world of fragmented living, competitiveness, pressure. Our refuge from a world that demands, and continues to demand. Our harbour of calm and peace in a world where silence has become alien; unwelcome, uninvited, unwanted. Our own Garden of Eden, providing all our needs, holding us in a dynamic, pulsating, vibrant support mechanism.

The awesome beauty that surrounds us! The magical, mystical wonder that Nature, in all its glory, exudes! Nature bearing testimony to the splendour, the magnificence, the grandeur of creation! The hand of God has moulded, sculpted and painted a Divine masterpiece in a wild, abandoned extravaganza of form, colour and texture.

The call of the Elemental Kingdoms is strong; beckoning us, urging us, enticing us to partake of its exotic elixir, its refreshing cocktail, its alluring charms.

God energy finds expression through everything in Nature; everything in Nature is infused with the Spirit of God. The power and might of God Essence is in the thunder; the intricate design of a bird's nest; the uniqueness of every leaf, every flower, every tree; migrating birds hitching a lift on the hot air currents; starlings flying in formation of the figure eight, the Infinity sign,- all testify to the instincts with which all of God's creatures are endowed. The night firmaments display creation's infinity and vastness with all the invisible workings behind them; the stars and planets alive with vibrating movement; Nature's purity and innocence irrefutable evidence of the unconditional love of God for all creatures and their total inclusiveness in God energy.

Sadly, many of us are oblivious to all we are being offered. And not just oblivious. We have encroached upon Nature's territory; we have destroyed; we have extracted; we have burned; we have exhausted and depleted all the natural resources that Mother Earth has so generously given, and continues to give. We grasp all and give nothing back.

There is an intelligence in all living things; God Intelligence. We are all part of an over-all, great collective Intelligence that seeks to express itself in many realities and in many forms. The hand of God, the beauty and the magnificence of creation is imbued into every life-form. Every rock and mountain, every river and ocean, every flower, every blade of grass, every tree and plant, every animal, bird and insect,- all are infused with the Spirit of God, all are intelligent forms of creation, resplendent in their uniqueness. And all with a greater understanding of their purpose than we humans; we humans who are limited by our denial of the existence of other forms of life around us other than what we can perceive and experience with our five physical senses.

Nature is vibrant, pulsating, a living miracle, offering us love; teaching us lessons; giving us pleasure; healing us.

And for what does Nature ask in return?

In return for all that Nature gives us, Nature asks only for acknowledgement, respect and love. That's all!

It is through Nature that God speaks to us! And the great writers, poets and artists heard and listened! And then they shared with us what they learned!

The great writers, poets and artists down through the centuries have acknowledged Nature's grandeur and beauty. But since the days of the industrial and agrarian revolutions, Nature has been disappearing from our awareness as we find ourselves caught up in the deceiving allure of materialism and self-gratifying pursuits.

Nature is our greatest teacher. Nature holds the key to our understanding of the meaning of life and death through the yearly cycle of the seasons. All life-forms exist in a perpetual, on-going rhythm of cycles. The grand time clocks of Nature usher in the seasons one after the other in an ordered, regimented pattern. Nature shows us how to go with the flow, to bend with the wind, to ride the storms, to grow towards the light. The flowers themselves nod and sway in time with the wind's gentle, carressing tune, perfectly harmonised. Nature teaches us to not worry, everything we need will manifest for us in a loving universe that knows our every desire and need, and will deliver.

William Wordsworth, one of the best known amongst a great array of poets, expressed the whole meaning of life in his poetry; the meaning of life as shown to him through Nature.

Wordsworth was born in Cumbria, in the Lake District, one of the most beautiful parts of England, in 1770. One of the Romantic poets, the name by which those who extolled the beauty of Nature are known, Wordsworth grew up surrounded by the beauty of the natural setting of the Lake District, and in total alignment with the vibrational energies of the Elemental Kingdoms.

For Wordsworth, Nature was his nurse, referring to *'Her'* throughout all of his poetry. He found delight and joy in a *'Field of golden daffodils'*, personified to emphasise the vital life-force running through them, as they *'danced'* and *'nodded'* their heads in a joyous expression of life.

He found excitement and thrills in skating across the ice on a darkening winter evening, in what he called "*A time of rapture*", where "*The stars / Eastward were sparkling clear, and in the west / The orange sky of evening died away*", as he "*Stood and watched / Till all was tranquil as a dreamless sleep*". Likewise, in the "*Act of stealth and troubled pleasure*" of stealing the boat to go out on the lake, where, "On *either side / Small circles glittering idly in the moon / Until they melted all into one track / Of sparkling light*", totally enraptured him.

Wordsworth did not just extol the beauty of Nature, but he was also pre-occupied with the moral effect of Nature, the lessons Nature has for us; a moral teacher, drawing his material from source, from Nature. In '*The World is too much with us*', Wordsworth explains how "*We lay waste our powers / Little we see in Nature that is ours; / We have given our hearts away, a sordid boon!*"

In '*Composed upon Westminster Bridge*', he admires the beauty of the stillness of London, at One wth Nature in the early hours of the morning, before the smoke and smog of the great city have begun to destroy and suffocate the awe-inspiring scene: "*Dull would he be of soul who could pass by / A sight so touching in its majesty / This City now doth, like a garment, wear / The beauty of the morning*".

Wordsworth's philosophies of life are clearly expounded in his '*Ode to Intimations of Immortality*'. Here, he explains how "*Our birth is but a sleep and a forgetting: / The Soul that rises with us, our life's Star, / Hath had elsewhere its setting,/ And cometh from afar: / Not in entire forgetfulness,/ And not in entire nakedness,/ But trailing clouds of glory do we come / from God, who is our home.*"

Through all his life, Wordsworth felt the connection with "*That imperial palace whence he came*" and how, at the same time, "*The homely Nurse doth all she can / To make her foster-child, her inmate Man, / Forget the glories he hath known.*"

Spirit Calling - Are You Listening?

Wordsworth understood all about the veil of forgetfulness pulled down over our eyes at birth, making us forget our existence in Spirit, in order for us to be able to experience life in this earth vibration. Nevertheless, he also understood that we can still access other higher vibrational levels while here on the earth plane: "*Though inward far we be,/ Our souls have sight of that immortal sea / Which brought us hither, / Can in a moment travel thither*".

Wordsworth absorbed all of Nature, from the "*Innocent brightness of a new-born Day*", to the lessons Nature is teaching us.

The poet John Keats, born in 1795, and like Wordsworth, one of the Romantic poets, those who extolled the beauty of Nature, captured the beauty and essence of autumn and the sense of Oneness with Nature in his famous '*Ode to Autumn*'.

An ode is a form of praise addressed directly to the object of the speaker's affections. Keats personifies autumn, creating the sights, sounds and textures through sensuous images. Autumn is directly addressed *as 'Thy'* and '*Thou*', a Goddess, with voluptuous beauty and abundance, a Goddess who '*conspires*' with the Sun, to "*load and bles'*", to "*bend*" the trees with apples and fruit, to "*swell the gourd and plump the hazel shells*".

The Deified season of autumn is a time of warmth and plenty, but it is perched on the shoulder of winter's desolation, as the bees enjoy "*later flowers*", the harvest is gathered from the fields, the lambs are now "*fully grown*", and the swallows gather for their winter migration.

In the face of the pending chill of winter, the late warmth of autumn provides ample beauty to celebrate: the cottage and its surroundings; the agrarian haunts of the Goddess and the locales of natural creatures. In '*To Autumn*', the sense of coming loss that permeates the poem confronts the sorrow that underlies the season's creativity. When autumn's harvest is over, the fields will be bare, the swaths with their "*twined flowers*" cut down, the cider-press dry, the skies empty. But the connection of this harvesting to the seasonal cycle softens the edge of the tragedy. In time, spring will come again, the fields will grow again, and the birdsong will return. What makes '*To Autumn*' beautiful is that it brings an acceptance of the cycle of life. Autumn is teaching us that re-birth will follow death in a natural cycle.

No wonder then that this "*season of mists and mellow fruitfulness*" bows out in a grand finale; a grand display of extravagant costumes; a final celebration of life before its long season of hibernation and renewing. It is the final encore, that final demand for attention, for acknowledgement, for recognition, in the undulating, seductive extravaganza of the final stage performance. For now!

The beauty of autumn is captured also in R. S. Thomas' poem '*A Day in Autumn*', and the memory of that scene will stay in the poet's mind, cheering him up in the long winter months, '*in the long cold*'. He lets his mind "*take its photograph*" after he has "*looked up/ From the day's chores*" to take in the beauty of "*A few last/ Leaves adding their decoration/ To the trees' shoulders, braiding the cuffs/ Of the boughs with gold; a bird preening/ In the lawn's mirror.*"

R. S. Thomas was born in 1913. A lot of his poetry is imbued with an understanding of man's connection and relationship with Nature. In '*Soil*', Thomas explores the importance of the earth, the soil, to man: "*The soil is all*". We are of the earth, and we will return to the earth. The farmer in Thomas' poem cannot see beyond his field; it is the only place he is "*free*". In the cycle of life, he will return to the soil. At the end of the poem, the farmer cuts himself and watches as his blood returns to the earth: "*Out of the wound the blood seeps home/ To the warm soil from which it came.*" Nature is man; man is Nature. There is no separateness.

Thomas' poem 'Farm Child ', portrays a young boy who lives on a farm,

Spirit Calling - Are You Listening?

and whose world revolves around Nature. He is at one with the life-forces around him: "*His head is stuffed with all the nests he knows.*" His pockets are full of "*Flowers/ Snail-shells and bits of glass, the fruit of hours/ Spent in the fields by thorn and thistle tuft.*" His treasures! The final line: "*Earth breeds* and beckons", sums up Thomas' belief, yet again, that we are more comfortable with Nature than we can ever be with materialism, to which so many of us are falsely attracted.

In '*Cynddylan on a Tractor*', Thomas shows how a mechanical machine is disturbing the peace and tranquillity of the rural area, and how the man is losing his connection with Nature, as machines now connect with the soil instead of man connecting through manual work. He is a "*new man now*", the gears of the tractor "*obeying his least bidding*", as he rides out of the farm-yard "*scattering chickens*" and "*emptying the wood/ Of foxes and squirrels and bright jays*". He is so caught up with the new machine that he no longer even notices how "*the sun comes over the tall trees*", or how "*all the birds are singing, bills open in vain.*" He has lost touch with Nature, and his life will be the more poorly for it. If there are benefits to the farmer through the new machines, it will come at a great expense to Nature. The poem is a clear message to all mankind that Nature will disappear from our perception if we force our will upon it instead of being at One with it.

Gerard Manley Hopkins, born in 1844, and in many ways the most remarkable poet of the Victorian period, imbued his poetry with strong and energetic energy, creating a musicality that bombards the senses . Hopkins truly saw how : "*This world is charged with the grandeur of God!*"

Hopkins' poem '*Pied Beauty*' is a song of praise, "*Glory be to God*", for everything in Nature that exemplifies the beauty of God with its colour and vibrancy: "*Finches' wings/ Landscape plotted and pieced- fold, fallow and plough/ And all trades, their gear and tackle and trim.*"

All this beauty is the hand of God: *"He fathers forth whose beauty is past change;/ Praise Him."*

Again, he brings musicality to Nature in '*Inversnaid*': *"Degged with dew, dappled with dew/ Are the groins of the braes that the brook treads through/ Wiry heathpacks, flinches of fern/ And the beadbonny ash that sits over the burn."*

He describes the natural scene in an extended mataphor: *"This darksome burn, horseback brown, / His rollrock highroad roaring down, / in coop and in comb the fleece of his foam / Flutes and low to the lake falls home."*

Hopkins is depicting a beautiful landscape, and then he reflects on it in the last lines: *"O let them be left, wildness and wet;/ Long live the weeds and the wilderness yet."*

A plea from Hopkins for preservation of the natural settings!

In '*Spring and Fall*', Hopkins embodies a profound idea. A child stands alone in a wood sadly watching the leaves fall: *"Margaret, are you grieving/ Over Goldenwood unleaving?"* The poet says that as she grows up, she will not have the same intense feelings for mere leaves; yet she will weep, but for her own state. Whatever we call it, all sorrow springs from the one source, which we cannot express, but only understand intuitively: *"Now no matter, child, the name:/ Sorrow's springs are all the same."* The falling of the leaves is also metaphorical for the transience of life, the ' *Fall*' in the title being symbolic of the autumn of our lives: *"It is the blight man was born for,/ It is Margaret you mourn for."*

The lessons Nature is teaching us!

In the sonnet '*Spring*', Hopkins vividly describes the lush growth of the new season: *"Nothing is so beautiful as Spring/ When weeds, in wheels, shoot long and lovely and lush;/ Thrush's eggs look like little low heavens, and*

Spirit Calling - Are You Listening?

thrush/ Through the echoing timber does so rinse and wring/ The ear, it strikes like lightnings to hear him sing."

Hopkins describes how: *"The glassy peartree leaves and blooms, they brush/ The descending blue; that blue is all in a rush/ With richness; the racing lambs too have fair their fling."*

However, in the last lines, Hopkins relates spring to the innocence of the Garden of Eden and of children before they are " *soured with sinning.*"

Hopkins was only one of the numerous poets who saw the beauty and the lessons in Nature.

Thomas Hardy, born in Dorset in 1840, was another such poet. In his poem *'The Darkling Thrush'*, which he wrote on the last day of the nineteenth century, Hardy is describing a desolate and dreary scene, reflecting his own gloom and isolation. In the depths of winter, *"The land's sharp features seemed to be/ The Century's corpse outleant,/ His crypt the cloudy canopy, /The wind his death-lament."*

The landscape is dead all around him: *"The ancient pulse of germ and birth/ Was shrunken hard and dry,/ And every spirit upon earth/ Seemed fervourless as I."*

Yet, in the midst of all this doom and gloom, an old thrush, *"frail, gaunt and small"*,   began to sing, and made Hardy consider that there was *"some blessed Hope, whereof he knew/ And I was unaware."*

An optimistic message for Hardy from the thrush, giving him hope for the new century, in the midst of all the dreariness and darkness around him!

This acknowledgement by Hardy that the animal kingdoms know more than we humans do is also referred to by William Wordsworth in his poem *'To a Skylark'*.

Wordsworth refers to the skylark as "*Ethereal minstrel*" and "*Pilgrim of the sky*", a creature of a higher mind, of a higher intelligence, that lives between two planes, and which "*dost pour upon the world a flood/ Of harmony, with instinct more divine;/ Type of the wise who soar, but never roam;/ True to the kindred points of Heaven and Home!*"

William Butler Yeats found a message in the swans on the lake in '*The Wild Swans at Coole*'. He considers how, as a species, the swans will live on after he dies; their beauty will remain, whereas he, by contrast, is ageing and fading. He feels he is losing the energy and love of life that the swans still possess: "*Their hearts have not grown old;/ Passion or conquest, wander where they will, / Attend upon them still*".

Yeats paints a picture of serenity and beauty around the swans on the lake in the autumnal setting, representative of the autumn of his own life: "*The trees are in their autumn beauty/ The woodland paths are dry,/ Under the October twilight the water/ Mirrors a still sky*".

In his famous poem '*The Lake Isle of Innisfree*', Yeats yearns for the peace and quiet that only Nature can offer, away from the "*pavements grey*" of London. In contrast, he will escape to Innisfree, where "*Midnight's all a glimmer, and noon a purple glow/ And evening full of the linnet's wings*".

Yeats' needs and philosophy of life are expounded in this musical poem, with the mixture of poetic descriptions of a beautiful place and the ear listening to nature. The musicality is achieved with the repeated soft vowel sounds interspersed with consonants: "*I will arise and go now, and go to Innisfree*".

The last line of the poem emphasises how deeply Yeats yearns for the silence and peace that he knows he will find only in Nature; constantly, while in London Nature calls to him: "*I hear it in the deep heart's core*".

Spirit Calling - Are You Listening?

This intoxicating love of Nature is shared by Patrick Kavanagh, a County Monaghan poet, in *'Shancoduff '*, a poem about his local area, where *"the sleety winds fondle the rushy beards of Shancoduff "*, and where these hills mean so much to him: *"they are my Alps and I have climbed the Matterhorn/ With a sheaf of hay for three perishing calves/ In the field under the Big Forth of Rocksavage."*

Robert Frost was an American poet, born in San Francisco in 1875 and at the age of ten went to live in New England, the area which inspired almost all of his poetry. His poems reflect a mind deeply connected with outdoor pursuits in an agrarian natural setting: mowing; mending walls; harvesting; apple-picking; clearing up fallen leaves.

In *'Mowing'*, Frost is aware of the sound of the scythe and ponders: *"What was it it whispered?"* In *'Mending Wall '*, he considers the whole reasoning behind building walls between himself and his neighbour: *"There where it is we do not need the wall;/ He is all pine and I am all apple orchard./ My apple trees will never get across/ And eat the cones under his pines, I tell him."*

In *'Dust of Snow'*, he portrays the consolations that Nature offers to human anxiety or misery, and how, through the simple experience of a crow shaking snow down on him from a tree, *"Has given my heart/ A change of mood/ And saved some part/ Of a day I had rued"*.

A transitory moment of pure delight in contemplation of the beauty of snow-covered woods, before he continues with his duties, is captured in *'Stopping by Woods on a Snowy Evening'*: *"The woods are lovely, dark and deep"*, and *"the only other sound's the sweep / Of easy wind and downy flake"*.

A similar moment of delight is found in *'Unharvested'*, when he unexpectedly comes across an apple tree that has shed its load of apples, symbolic of the joys we find in unexpected places, and outside of our ordinary every-day routine: *"May something go always unharvested/*

May much stay out of our stated plan/ Apples or something forgotten and left/ So smelling their sweetness would be no theft".

Yes, Nature has certainly given us much to think about!

What lessons these poets all learned, what beauty they all saw in Nature! What peace and serenity they found there! What healing and nurturing they experienced!

Even in the depths of austere winter, Nature continues to exude its beauty and charms, continues to depict in front of us the Grand Design for earth, continues to remind us that we are all part of the same Divine Consciousness, all inter-related, all inter-connected in the vastness of creation.

The magical, crystal fairy-land that earth becomes when dressed in her winter coat! The fantasy-land of sparkling, radiating whiteness and purity! The majestic, elegant grandeur of her gleaming coat of shimmering icing! The ice-blue mountain peaks, capped in snow, penetrating the hypnotic depths of an azure blue sky! The blanket of white draped around her shoulders; the shimmering, sparkling, dancing effervescence in the luminous rays of the moonbeams! The virgin carpet of immaculate white! A masterpiece, frozen in time! A mirage, captured in the still reflection of ice-encrusted waters! The tiny, twirling, glittering snowflakes in free fall, meandering lazily in their descent to earth! The eerie, other-worldly hush that lies over everything, echoing from every tree and sleeping life-form. In the stillness, in the hush, in the echoing, velvety, deafening quiet, there is a lesson to be learned. The lesson that winter is a time of resting, replenishing, renewing, before the call of spring awakens all life to another round of birth, life and then death once again; another stage performance where Nature's costumes become more elaborate, more eye-catching, more extravagant as the year progresses. After her long winter sojourn, Nature again bursts onto the scene, more resplendent, more passionate, more intoxicating, more all-consuming, re-energised after the long hibernation, ready to dazzle and sparkle, dance and sing, strut and flirt, teach and heal.

Nature is here for us all. Nature is here to embrace us all in its healing balm; to cocoon us all in a gentle, soothing blanket of love and compassion; to enfold us all in a loving embrace, nurturing, replenishing, renewing; teaching us lessons; helping us all along our path; supporting us, encouraging us; and above all, healing us.

What a gift Spirit has given to us in Nature!

And all we have to do is accept and show appreciation for that gift; all we have to do is notice the splendour and beauty around us; all we have to do is respect the Elemental Kingdoms that co-exist alongside us on a different vibrational level, pouring their Spirit into the plants and flowers, the trees and the rivers. The Spirit that every living thing holds within it, the life-force that exists within us all, animal, human, vegetable and mineral!

Just like us, the trees and flowers change in outwardly appearance. And just like us, the same life-force lives within; immortal, eternal, unending.

We are connected to Nature with an umbilical cord; but, unlike the umbilical cord that attaches the babe in the womb to the mother and is disconnected at birth, the umbilical cord that attaches us to Nature can never be disconnected or broken. Nature, as Wordsworth said, is our *'Nurse'*, our *'Mother'*, continuously nurturing, replenishing, nourishing us. And healing us; mostly healing us!

And whatever love we give to Nature, we will get all that returned to us again a hundred-fold!

Surely an offer we cannot refuse!

EXERCISE

HEALING PLANET EARTH

- *Sit comfortably, back straight*

- *Ground and protect*

- *Take three deep breaths to connect with Universal Energy*

- *When you are ready, visualise yourself holding the Earth between the palms of your hands*

- *Feel the Earth rotating slowly in your hands*

- *As it rotates, visualise White Light going out from your third eye and Pink Light going out from your heart to the Earth, filling it with healing and love*

- *Now visualise the Earth becoming still, and whatever part of the Earth you see when it stops rotating, that is the area that urgently needs healing at this moment in time*

- *Intensify the White Light and the Pink Light you are sending to this area*

- *When you are ready, let the Earth begin to rotate again, and allow it to stop again wherever it so chooses. Again, send intensified Light to this area*

- *Continue to watch the Earth rotate and stop for as long as you wish, sending strong White and Pink Light to those particular areas*

CHAPTER 8

SLEEP ON IT!

Sleep is a necessary and vital part of our life. It would need to be, as we spend so much of our time actually doing it! Over one-third of our life-time actually! So it would need to be worth it!

It is only on planet earth that sleep applies. Humans, animals, even the flowers and trees require sleep, due to the dense energy here, unlike other higher forms of energy vibration, which do not require sleep.

Shakspeare's Macbeth explains sleep for us: *"Sleep that knits up the ravelled sleave of care/ The death of each day's life, sore labour's bath/ Balm of hurt minds, great nature's second course/ Chief nourisher in life's feast."*

So, if sleep is such a vital part of our life, what exactly does it do for us? What is its function? What actually happens when we sleep?

When we sleep, we dream. Dreams are not just a form of free in-house entertainment. Nor is sleep just a time of nourishment and rest for our physical body! Far from it!

In order to understand what happens when we sleep, we need to understand that we have two minds: the conscious mind and the subconscious mind.

And what exactly is the difference between the conscious mind and the subconscious mind?

Picture an iceberg. An iceberg has two parts: the small visible part above the water and the greater part which lies below the water. Just like our conscious and subconscious minds! The small part of the iceberg above the water represents our conscious mind; the greater part of the iceberg below the water represents our subconscious mind.

Our conscious mind is responsible for all of our actions and thoughts while we are in the wakened state. It controls all our thinking, our movements, all that we do by intention while being conscious. It is logical and reasoning; it is a place of cognitive learning and understanding; it solves problems; it makes choices based on facts and moves the body deliberately. For example, when we move an arm, a leg, a hand, then that is done by the conscious mind. It also acts as a gate-keeper for the mind, filtering criticism or diverting negative, poisonous arrows aimed at us by others.

The subconscious mind, on the other hand, is responsible for all our involuntary actions: our breathing; our kidneys; our liver function; our heart rate. It operates below the level of our normal consciousness. And it is this subconscious mind that is in charge of our emotions. Our deepest beliefs are programmed into our subconscious mind.

While the awakened state is the natural state for our conscious mind, sleep is the natural state for our subconscious mind. Once we fall asleep, our mind switches on to auto-pilot and the subconscious mind takes over.

The subconscious mind has no programming mechanism of its own. It receives and downloads all that is fed into it from the conscious mind. It accepts as true everything that the conscious mind tells it. It cannot discriminate between our true feelings and our pretend or false feelings; it has absolutely no sense of humour. So if, for example, you feed it the idea that you are ill, or that you are in poverty, the subconscious mind absorbs that feeling and manifests it.

Your subconscious mind never changes what you feed into it. It can't! It doesn't know how!

All your subconscious mind is capable of doing is absorbing what you download into it, and then making that manifest.

Spirit Calling - Are You Listening?

Your subconscious mind responds to feelings; nothing else.

So, following all this through logically, whatever you wish to manifest in your life, therefore, you must first feel it, and then impress it onto your subconscious mind, where it will be manifested.

During sleep, you enter the world of the subconscious mind. It is during sleep that your conscious mind leaves the limiting world of your five physical senses and surrenders to your subconscious mind. And remember! Your subconscious mind always responds to your conscious mind, no matter what your conscious mind has fed it. It takes its impressions and instructions only from your conscious mind. Nothing, absolutely nothing else, can make any impact whatsoever on your subconscious mind.

So sleep, being the natural state for your subconscious mind, is the place where all the planning, all the thought-processing, all the ideas are put together to make your life run smoothly, or not-so-smoothly, depending on what you have fed into your subconscious mind just before you fall asleep.

Those few moments before you drift off into the world beyond your five physical senses, therefore, are the most important moments of your day. It is from here that you control what happens in your life.

The world beyond your five physical senses is an unlimited, creative, imaginative landscape, where you can experience anything. Anything! Here, literally, is the world of your dreams. In this other-world you experience timelessness, wish-fulfilment, miracles, with no sense of boundaries or linear progression.

So now you can see that whatever you feed into your subconscious mind just before you drift off into the sleeping state, needs to be positive, productive and life-enhancing. If you go to sleep thinking of all the woes that befell you during the day, all the ills and pains you

61

experienced, all the slights you received, all the poor-me feelings, then what you are doing is programming your subconscious mind to manifest all of that on a multiplied scale the next day!

If, on the other hand, you fall off to sleep thinking of all the good things, all the positive things, all the happy thoughts you had, all the wonderful things you would like to happen to you, then that is what you are feeding into your subconscious mind, and your subconscious mind goes to work on it immediately. Surely that is good news!

And there is even better news! You don't have to wait until you fall asleep to programme your subconscious mind to manifest for you what you want! Meaning?

Ever heard of day-dreaming?

When we day-dream, our mind goes to auto-pilot; our subconscious takes over and feeds on what our conscious mind has downloaded into it. And you now know how this will work out! So how can you ever say that day-dreaming is a waste of time? That time you have just spent day-dreaming could indeed prove to be the most productive part of your day! And you had absolutely no physical exertion or active input from your physical body! What's not to like about all that?

Indeed, as the poet, Emily Dickenson, wrote in '*A Long, Long Sleep*': "*Was ever idleness like this?*" Certainly worth thinking about!

Yes, your subconscious mind can be easily trained to obey your every wish, your every command! Easy! I have never owned or used an alarm clock. All I have ever done is tell my subconscious mind before I go to sleep the time at which I want wakened. Sometimes I just visualise the hands of the clock in a certain position, and then I drift off. Again, when I forget something, I just tell my subconscious mind to remind me about it in the morning. All I can say is that my subconscious mind has never yet let me sleep in or failed to remind me! Try it! Literally, just sleep on it!

What else happens when we sleep?

When we sleep, our soul '*Astral-Travels*'.

In each incarnation that we undertake, we do not bring all of our soul with us. And why not? Simply because we do not need all of our soul in each incarnation, only a miniscule part for each life-time. The greater part of our soul remains with Spirit, and that is what we call our Higher Self. Our Higher Self knows absolutely everything there is to know. It has unlimited knowledge, unlike our soul part that accompanies us here, which has only limited knowledge. And why has that soul part only got limited knowledge? Because we do not need to know everything this time around, or any time around. We have come here to learn lessons in order to evolve as Spiritual beings and further our Spiritual evolution. Hence the veil of amnesia pulled down over us once we move into the Vibrational Corridor to enter this earth plane. The soul part we bring with us, however, does not particularly enjoy being confined and trapped in our physical body; it is meant to fly freely. And that is exactly what it does when we sleep!

When we enter sleep mode, our soul leaves our body and astral-travels to join its greater other part in Spirit, to enjoy the freedom, the Oneness, the joy of just being in Spirit again. It is a welcome temporary sojourn from entrapment in a heavy-vibratioal, dense-energy physical body. A welcome release from the earth plane back to its normal, natural state!

So sleep is not just a time for our physical body to receive nourishment, replenishment and re-energising. It is a time for our soul to rejoin its greater part and re-energise in that Spiritual energy and love.

And there' s more!

It is when we are in our state of sleep that higher vibrational energies can make contact with us, simply because we are totally relaxed, chilled out, accessible. Our loved ones who have already passed back to Spirit can get through to us on our sleep frequency wave; those higher vibrational beings who wish to interact with us can merge with us and impress their presence on our subconscious mind. We are given messages in our dreams, all metaphorical of course. So if, for example, we dream of a death, it does not mean that person is about to die. Rather, death is symbolic of new beginnings, the end of some phase in our life, the closing of some particular door, or whatever.

The poet, John Keats, in his poem 'Sleep' writes: "Turn the key deftly in the oiled words/ And seal the hushed casket of my soul." And again: "O soft embalmer of the still midnight/ Shutting, with careful fingers and benign/ Our gloom-pleas'd eyes, embower'd from the light/ Enshaded in forgetfulness strive/ O soothest sleep!"

And finally, Shakespeare's Hamlet yearned for the solace and escape that sleep brings: "To sleep, to sleep, perchance to dream."

For surrendering just over one-third of our life-time to sleep, we certainly experience and gain a lot in return! We receive not only healing and nourishment for our physical body, but also healing, nourishment and re-energising for our soul. Sleep heals us physically, Spiritually and emotionally.

No wonder babies sleep so much! They have just left the Spirit world and so are all still pure light, uncontaminated as yet by the ways of this world. Your dog sleeps a lot too! Again, a being of pure light!

There must be something in it!

CHAPTER 9

PRAYER AND MEDITATION: GOING WITHIN

There is a world-wide belief in the efficacy of prayer; a world-wide belief in praying to a God who sometimes grants our requests and sometimes does not, all for our own highest good. If we do not get what we asked God for, then it was not for our own good that God should grant that particular request.

We have been taught to pray in the belief that prayer is powerful; prayer can move mountains.

And yes, the power of prayer is indeed great! But perhaps not exactly in the way we have been led to believe!

What is prayer?

Prayer is simply a means of communicating with God.

Unfortunately, however, prayer for most of us is usually an intermittent, glibly rhymed-off pattern of words taught to us from our childhood. We prattle away, uttering learned phrases, while at the same time probably thinking of all sorts of things to do in our busy, hectic lives. Then we get a sense of relief from having handed over whatever it was we were praying for. This mechanical repetition of learned words in the form of a prayer in order to fulfill some particular religious obligation is NOT prayer!

And when do we usually pray? Usually when we want something! And what form does our prayer usually take? A beseeching, an imploring, an asking for some particular favour from a deity on high.

This is NOT what prayer should be all about! Our whole life should be, and is, a prayer! Prayer is living, celebrating the joy of life, of just being! Prayer should NOT be something we squeeze somewhere into our busy, crammed, hectic schedule! We just cannot connect with Source in this way. We cannot connect with Source if our mind is busy, busy, busy.

Prayer should NOT always be an asking process, a begging, a cry for help. Something we turn to when all else fails!

We need to understand what prayer really is! We need to re-think our attitude towards prayer!

And yet again, we need to get the truth!

To arrive at the truth about prayer, to understand what prayer is, we need to understand the nature of God and the fact that everything, including God, is energy. And here is where meditation becomes relevant.

Prayer and meditation are both forms of communication with the God energy. Prayer is active; meditation is passive.

Prayer is the individual's action of speaking to Source; meditation is the individual's action of remaining in silence, the inaction of listening to the voice of Spirit speaking. So, while prayer, on the one hand, is speaking to Spirit, meditation, on the other hand, is listening to Spirit, listening to our own inner voice, the God energy within ourselves, the God energy within our own being, our own Higher Self.

Prayer, as we mostly practise it, is an outward projection, outward from the individual to some external force that we believe exists outside of ourselves; some external force that we believe will grant our request, our application. It is a surrendering of our own control to a higher force we think will handle the situation for us, that will, in a

Spirit Calling - Are You Listening?

way, wave a magic wand and solve the problem.

Meditation is a movement inwards; inwards towards our own Divine Source, our own Divine Essence, our own Divine nature, our Higher Self, which has all the answers to all the questions we could ever ask. In meditation we merge our own Divine nature, our own energy, with the God energy, the energy that is within ourselves, and we draw from that energy, we call forth from that energy whatever we desire.

We need to realise and understand that what we are seeking does NOT lie outside of ourselves, but within our own heart, deep in our own Divine Spirit. *"Heaven lies within"* we have been told! But what does this all mean? How do we go within?

In order to go within, we need silence. In order to obtain silence, we need to calm our thinking and activities; we need to be peaceful.

Meditation is the process of learning to be silent, to calm our thinking and activities so that we can pause and rest for a while within that silence, within that calmness.

And in this peace and silence established through meditation, the individual makes a one-to-one contact with Source, with one's own inner self.

All of life is simply energy, vibrating at particular and various frequencies. Energy vibrating at certain frequencies produces physical manifestations in the form of objects, situations, circumstances and events.

Energy is like a magnet, attracting other energies to it. The universe feels your energy, and whatever energy you put out into the universe will attract similar energy from the universe back to you.

What has all this got to do with prayer and meditation?

The reality is that certain circumstances, certain events, certain people enter our lives for reasons other than that we prayed to God for them to materialise.

The reality is that God neither grants nor denies the prayers of anyone.

The reality is that we do not need to supplicate God for manifestations in our lives. And why not? Because we ourselves need to take responsibility for our own lives, we ourselves need to apply the power of God in our lives, not supplicate God to apply this power for us!

The reality is that we ourselves are God Essence. So when we pray to God we are actually addressing our own Higher Self, that inner Spiritual part of us that knows all the answers.

Remember! Everything, including God, is energy! We are inherent in that Divine energy, not outside it. It is the God energy, our own energy, that manifests our requests. And what we need to do is tap into that source of energy for ourselves!

When we pray, our thoughts become energy, attracting similar energy back to us from the universe. If we fear something, then the energy we send out in the form of fear attracts more of that to us. If we send out love, then that too attracts similar energy to us. When we ask for something to materialise in our lives, what we are actually doing is sending out the thought, the feeling, the energy that we do not have that particular object in our lives right now. See what's happening here? The universe always agrees with us! So when we send out vibes, energy, thoughts declaring that we lack something, then we are creating that lack as our reality!

Now, if we change our prayer terminology, just place a different slant on it all; just affirm that we already have what we request, then the universe agrees and materialises more of the same! What we have done here is simply tap in to the great universal wheel of energy, the great God energy, selecting what we want from it! So instead of saying *"Dear God, please give me good health"*, say instead,*"Dear God, thank you for my good health,"* or better still, *"I now have a good health consciousness"*. Remember! Thoughts create results; affirmations change results. The former is a request, a supplication, an inadvertent admission that something is conspicuously absent from our lives; the latter is an affirmation, a confirmation, an acknowledgement, an expression of gratitude that the required outcome already exists. As it does! It already exists, as everything, past, present, future, exists, in the God energy. All we need to do is call it forth!

Meditation is aligning yourself with the universal energy, the God energy.

In meditation, we connect with the God energy more easily. We cannot connect with higher vibrational energies, never mind the highest vibrational energy of all, if our mind is busy, busy, busy.

There are three parts to us: body, mind and soul.

The physical body is merely the temporary vehicle by means of which we transport our immortal soul through this life-time. If we believe our physical body is all there is to us, then we will fail to access the whole fabric of life, the whole wonder of life, outside of our five physical senses. We will simply drift along, at the mercy of whatever happens to come to us, a victim of fate, 'poor me' in a hostile, unfriendly, uncaring world.

If we accept that we are also a mind and a soul we will understand and accept that we are part of Divine, God energy.

Let me give you an example of how this all works!

Morning rush-hour. Everything is hectic. School uniform has just had egg deposited on it! Baby's nappy needs changing, again! Lunches are not yet ready. Everyone, including you, is in a tizzy! " *Hurry up! Get a move on! We're all going to be late!"*

Sounds familiar? Of course it does! Every house, every morning, every family!

Now, in such circumstances, you probably feel the urge to utter a desperate cry, a prayer, to God on High to settle all this, to help. "*Dear God! Give me patience!"* or "*Dear God! Give me strength!"*or even "*Dear God, get me to work on time!"*

BUT! Just hold on a minute here! Let's re-run all this!

You yourself, NOT God have got yourself into this tizzy. You yourself, NOT God, have brought all this on yourself! You yourself, NOT God, have sent out the wrong energy into the universe, and you know what has been happening! The universe has increased that energy and sent more of the same back to you! If you continue on as you are, you will only continue to attract even more of the same to you! You will have to contend with angry, frazzled drivers, red traffic lights, traffic jams; by the time you get the children to school, you will be like one of those electrocuted cartoon figures, hair standing out on end, all frazzled! Not to mention your head! And it will continue! It will continue until you get yourself out of that mess.

And you think that God will get you out of the mess that you, yourself, got yourself into, simply because you do not understand and accept this whole question of energy and how it all works!

So, if sending up a prayer into the ether is not the answer, what is? What do you, NOT God, need to do, to get this situation back in balance? It's perfectly obvious what you must do! You must change the energy around you! Change the energy that brought all this on in the first place! Praying to God won't do the trick! Changing the energy will!

And how do you change the energy?

You change the energy by going into quiet mode, into peaceful mode; re-aligning yourself with the energy of the universe; calming yourself; sending out calm, peaceful energy into the universe! And instead of pleading, "*Dear God, please get me to work on time!*" or "*Dear God, please help me here!*" say instead "*I am in my peaceful consciousness*". The few minutes that you take time out doing this will save you much more time in the long run! And just watch as the traffic lights turn green for you; the angry drivers avoid you,- your energy is not matching theirs, and therefore of no attraction to them; others let you sidle into the traffic! And God did NOT do any of this! You, yourself, did, by tapping into the universal energy, into your own higher self, to get the outcome you wanted!

Get the message?

Praying to God for a good exam result, for a new car or whatever else you might pray to God for, is NOT going to manifest your request! Prayer is a goal-directed activity, a wish out into the universe for a particular manifestation. If prayer, as we know it and practise it were the answer to everything, then think of how many times the words, "*God save the Queen*" are sent out into the universe! But like everyone else, the British monarch, like every other monarch will pass back to Spirit when the time is right! No amount of prayers are going to prevent that! Or if you arrive at the airport only to discover you have forgotten to bring your passport, then no amount of prayers, no matter how highly Spiritually evolved you are, is going to make your passport suddenly manifest!

It is, however, really a futile exercise to try to compare prayer and meditation. They are closely related; just different sides of the same coin, both ways of communicating with, tapping into the God energy.

Prayer however, as most of us recognise it and practise it, is mostly meaningless. That is because of our belief in the nature of prayer; our greatly mistaken belief.

Prayer, like meditation, should be contemplative, going inwards to the silence within ourselves, and not an outward show of insincere, repetitive rhymed words. Our communication with God energy should come from the heart, from sincere feelings of gratitude for everything we have. Prayer should be wordless; after all, words are the human method of communicating! But God is NOT a human being!

God is energy, and we are of that God energy. We can only tap into that God energy, we can only access that God energy in times of peace and quiet. In the peace and quiet, we listen to our own inner voice, we receive the messages we need to receive from our own higher self, the God energy within each one of us. It is through meditation that we arrive at this state of quiet and stillness, quiet calmness, where we are in receptive mode, where we get the answers from our own inner self, not from some external force we see as God.

Prayers are thoughts, and like all thoughts, they go out from us on different vibrations, magnetising back to us similar to what we have sent out. We, not an external God, are the source of our own reality. So instead of asking this external God for something, go into the silence within yourself, and search for the answer as to how you can best bring it about.

In the silence within, you will be led to a place of acceptance and understanding as to what you can change and what you cannot change, and you will have the wisdom to know the difference. You will have the wisdom to know how to flow with the universal energy, the God energy, and you will know that you, yourself, can call forth all you desire from that universal God energy, because, after all, you, yourself, are part of it!

We are all a manifestation of God energy. We *are* God energy and how we use that energy determines the kind of life we live. And prayer is simply the process of calling forth that God energy into the manifestation of what we desire. The entire process of praying is internal, going within our own being; a journey in consciousness; transferring the dense matter of the material world into invisible, but tangible energy.

And when we pray in groups or in large numbers, the combined vibration that goes out from us is much greater than that from an individual sending out thoughts on the vibration of prayer. When many of us are thinking and sending out the same thoughts, then there is a very high likelihood that those thoughts will manifest! But NOT because God will, once again, wave some sort of magic wand! It's all got to do with energy, and how the energy we send out magnetises similar energy to us!

A Spiritual person is not assessed by the amount of prayers he or she sends up into the Heavens. Rather, a Spiritual person is one who listens for the silent voices; one who observes the invisible objects; one who knows that God is within, in perfect communication, in perfect symmetry; one who sees through the eye of the soul.

A Spiritual person is able to reach beyond the material into that place within where there is a merging and a realisation that we and God are all One; there is no separateness.

We must all take responsibility for ourselves; we must believe in our own possibilities; we must acknowledge the power each of us has as a part of God energy! And in order to manifest anything, in order to achieve anything in life, a portion of that energy must be contacted and used. And it is how we use that energy that determines the kind of life we live!

So yes, pray! And continue to pray! And pray now as you have never prayed before! Literally!

Pray now in the knowledge that when you pray to God, you are NOT praying to some external force, some higher power outside of yourself who will grant or deny your request. Pray now in the knowledge that you are actually connecting with your own soul, your own Higher Self, your own God Essence, that part of you that knows all the answers to all the questions you could ever ask. You are tapping into your own Divine power; you are taking responsibility for your own life; you are getting guidance from your own inherent God Essence as to how you, yourself, can work towards the best outcome, how you, yourself, and not some external force, can work towards the best result. That is what is meant by '*going within*'. That is what is meant by '*Heaven lies within*'.

And when you pray to certain Saints, Ascended Masters, Angels or other higher vibrational energy forces, what exactly are you doing?

In this case, the process of praying is slightly different. These higher vibrational forces such as Jesus the Christ, Mother Mary or any of the Saints or Angels are form, unlike God, who is formless. When we try to picture saints or angels or Ascended Masters, we can get an image in our heads of what they may look like. But when we try to picture God? When we try to picture God, what image do we get? None! And that's because God is formless!

The Saints, Ascended Masters, Angels, all act as facilitators, to enable us to connect with our Higher Self more easily. They clear the pathway for us, strengthening our connection with our Higher Self. They are all beings existing on the highest vibrational levels, all intent on helping us here on the earth plane to raise our Spiritual consciousness, to become more Spiritually aware, to grow further towards Enlightenment. When we call on these beings of Light, we

Spirit Calling - Are You Listening?

are tapping into their energies, attracting their energies to us. And when we pray in large groups, the pull from us is even greater.

We can feel these higher vibrational energies too, at sacred sites. Sacred sites are where the physical and Spiritual worlds meet. Sacred sites are where there is a residue of energy still remaining from higher vibrational visitations to our earth plane. Sacred sites mostly lie along ley lines, which are the earth's energy lines, just like the chakras in the human body. Again, it's all explained through energy. The energy along the earth's ley lines is higher than the energy in other areas, and that higher energy makes an encounter with the highest energy levels more possible.

How often have you visited a place where an unhappy event has taken place? I remember how I felt when I visited Dachau Concentration Camp, many years ago. It was not just the absence of any birds singing that created the heaviness, that awful feeling that weighed me down, like a heavy weight clinging to me. That was the negative energy of the pain and suffering that took place there still hanging around. Likewise, when I recently visited the Killing Fields in Cambodia. The heavy, negative energy there still lingers, testimony to the horrors that were perpetrated on that spot.

Conversely, when we visit religious sites, we feel the powerful energies of love surround us like a cocooning blanket, warm, soothing, coming from the loving energies of the higher, vibrational energies that manifested there.

Prayer is our way of communicating with God and the higher, vibrational Spiritual forces. And in order for our prayers to be effective, we need to understand the nature of God and the nature of prayer. Prayers are personal to each one of us; prayers cannot be effective when we just rhyme off words learned from childhood; prayers are thoughts coming from the heart, and only when they come from the heart can they have any meaning.

And they can only have any meaning or be in any way effective when we understand the nature of God, the nature of prayer and what it means to pray.

Remember! Like everything else, praying has all got to do with energy, and attracting energy, and with understanding that when we pray to God, we are actually connecting with our own higher self, and NOT, as we have for so long been led to believe, some remote external force outside of our own being.

You want to see God? You want to see God face to face? You sure?

Just look in the mirror!

CHAPTER 10

CRYSTALS

Crystals and stones are of the earth, part of earth's treasures, some hidden deep beneath the surface, others openly exposed, but all exhibiting electrical or magnetic properties; all containing and concentrating the earth's energies.

The earth, like everything else, is part of the vast energy network that is all of creation and, within the earth's energies, crystals are living, vibrating forms of that energy, powerful tools which can enhance our lives and our world in so many ways.

Right down through history, even from the earliest pre-historic times, crystals have been used as a source of energy, a Spiritual energy generator and director. The mystic properties of crystals and stones were unquestioned. Gemstones have been carried or worn for thousands of years, not just for decoration, but for the life-sustaining properties they exude. They have been used for personal, environmental and multi-dimensional healing, and also for Spiritual alchemy, which is the changing of base metals into other substances.

In the Golden Age of Atlantis, crystals were used to generate power. A much more advanced civilisation than we here at present, millions of light years ahead of us in fact, the Atlanteans enjoyed amazing psychic powers, with communication systems and technology so far in advance of us that we cannot even begin to imagine what it was like. And the power for all of this was generated by the huge crystals from Mother Earth. That's how powerful crystals are!

Today, crystals are of increasingly great value, and everything from watches to telecommunications makes use of them.

A great unprecedented surge of interest and use of crystals is taking place. Why? Because the earth's vibration is changing! We are all changing! The years of controlling, suppressing religious structures have ended. As has too, the tight suffocating grip that materialism has had over us for so long. We have allowed ourselves to become estranged from Mother Earth, but now so many of us are once again feeling the pull of Nature, the pull of the natural earth.

Crystals are re-connecting us with the earth once more. We are using crystals for healing, for bringing us back into balance, for psychic work, to calm our hectic life styles, for meditation, to increase the energy in our homes and to protect us. We wear crystals in jewellery and birth stones which we see as symbolic of all the inter-planetary energies with which we are all connected.

Crystals as a source of energy transcend all religions. They are simply part of the energy of Source, the God energy that is in all of us.

Each of us is different in our energetic resonance, hence we are all attracted to different crystals, depending on what our particular needs are at any one time. When we are in a crystal shop, we probably find it all very confusing at first as to which crystal to choose. But the reality is, we do not choose the crystal; the crystal chooses us! Fact! When we run our hands above the various crystals we will feel ourselves being drawn to a particular crystal, and we then know that is the one for us. The energy of that particular crystal resonates with our energy, and magnetises us to it. Some of them will jump out at us immediately, letting us know they are for us!

Crystals go beyond time and space. They vibrate within a unified field of consciousness that continues to connect them wherever they are. They carry coded information, buried deep within the earth, to be revealed when the time is right. The awareness of this and of the healing properties of crystals has been incorporated into esoteric

Spirit Calling - Are You Listening?

knowledge from time immemorial. As we lost our connection with Source and with Mother Earth, we also lost our connection with crystals, with the crystal oversouls, that life-force that runs through them. Now, we are once again re-connecting with these powerful, mighty oversouls, as we are expanding our Spiritual consciousness, our Spiritual awareness. We are awakening to our Spiritual essence, we are aligning with other higher vibrations and the more we align with higher vibrational forces and the more we interact with other higher dimensions, the more we will have access to the coded information embedded within crystals. They hold the secrets of existence that will be revealed to us when we are ready to receive.

Crystals enable us to expand our consciousness, to increase our energy and to protect our energy field. They are for use in chakra work and in all forms of meditation and healing. They are particularly effective in grounding exercises. We need to be grounded in the earth plane, because if we are not, then whatever might happen in expanded awareness will have absolutely no relevance for us. We will just feel spaced out, unbalanced and eventually ill. Crystals provide grounding and a smooth transition between different levels of vibration.

Yes! Crystals are a living, vibrant form of energy!

Open your mind to the energy of crystals. Feel the energy from the crystal you hold in your hand; the tingling sensation that runs through your palms. Sense a particular crystal's energy calling to you from amongst all the other crystals on display in front of you. Feel the energy from a small stone calling to you as you walk alongside a stream or along the beach. Gently pick it up; it's yours; yours to keep. It has chosen you because it has a message for you. Perhaps it just wants to give you peace and comfort every time you hold it in your hands. Place crystals around your home and feel the peace and harmony they bring to your surroundings. Wear a piece of crystal jewellery or carry a small crystal or stone with you as you go about your daily business and feel the sense of calm it exudes, or maybe just the sense of companionship or protection.

Remember! Crystals are living, pulsating, vibrant! They are not innate objects just to be admired for their beauty. They are meant to assist us on our Spiritual journey, bringing light into our inner being, as they remind us, in the words of Chief Seattle, *"We are part of the Earth and the Earth is part of us"*.

EXERCISE - GROUNDING WITH CRYSTALS

- *Sit comfortably in an upright position, back straight, both feet firmly on the ground.*

- *Take three deep breaths .*

- *Now visualise roots, like roots of trees spreading downwards from the soles of your feet, down into Mother Earth, spreading outwards in all directions. Feel yourself making contact with Mother Earth and allow Mother Earth to uphold and support you.*

- *Further down below you, deep down inside the earth, you now see a large cave, full of crystals, sparkling, glittering.*

- *Visualise your roots now going further down into this cave*

- *Let your roots connect with whatever crystals you wish. There are crystals of all sizes, shapes and colours. Purple amethyst; clear quartz; pink rose quartz; smoky quartz; cloudy Madagascar quartz; yellow citrine; orange, grey and white calcite; blue agate; white and black moonstone; opal; gold; selenite; lapus lazuli; topaz; aragonite; jade, to name but a few.*

- *Concentrate on the crystals that attract you to them by their shape or colour.*

- *Feel your roots digging deep into these crystals, connecting with the crystal energy.*

- *Now breathe in deeply, and as you breathe in, draw up the crystal energy, up through the earth and into your feet, ankles, legs, right up through your entire body.*

- *As you exhale, visualise all the negative energy leaving your body; all your worries and problems returning to Mother Earth to be transmuted.*

- *Breathe in again, feeling the energy of the crystals fill your entire body; and as you exhale, send the negative energy and your worries from your body down into Mother Earth. Repeat once more.*

- *Now sit for a while enjoying the beauty and peace of the crystal energy.*

- *When you are ready, disconnect your roots from the crystals and slowly, gently, bring your roots back to your feet. Observe your breathing for a while, feeling the different sensations in your energy body.*

CHAPTER 11

MY TIME IN CHEROKEE INDIAN LAND

The Appalachian Mountains in North Carolina, including the Great Smoky Range and the Blue Ridge Mountains, estimated to be five hundred million years old, are among the most ancient and most biologically diverse eco systems in the world. They have been home to Native Americans for centuries, and the land still echoes with the energy of these indigenous peoples who lived close to Nature, embracing the beauty and magnificence of these majestic peaks, many of which rise to over 6,000 feet. The Blue Ridge Mountains Range, known to the Cherokee Indian as the *'land of the blue mist'*, 50 miles from Ashville, stretch away into remote horizons, their peaks mystically shrouded in a bluish smoke-like haze, due to the isoprene released into the atmosphere, rising from the dense plant growth.

Here, amidst these mountains, where time no longer exists, one encounters the two-legged, the four-legged and the winged. Flocks of wild turkey; grouse; herds of whitetail deer; the lone coyote; the American black bear; reptiles and snakes, all co-habit amongst the sloped forests of stunted oak, oak-hickory, pine, spruce, fir, cane, swaying oaks and sycamores that blanket the entire landscape, intertwined with grass, shrubs, ivy and hemlock. The chorus of diverse songbirds and humming-birds fills the air, the elusive white owl somewhere amongst them.

The 56,000 acre Cherokee Indian Reservation, home to over 10,000 members of the Eastern Band of the Cherokee, and now a tourist-oriented area, is located at the town of Cherokee at the entrance to The Great Smoky Mountains National Park and at the southern end of The Blue Ridge Parkway. The Oconaluftee Indian Village portrays an 18th century Cherokee Village on a large site on the mountainside

Spirit Calling - Are You Listening?

above the town of Cherokee. This is not just a place; it is a time warp, 1759. It is set amongst the natural beauty of streams, rhododendrons, pine, spruce and fir trees, with houses constructed of woven saplings plastered with mud, early log cabins and brush arbors. The air is permeated with the sweet intoxicating scent of woodsmoke. The ancient skills of hulling canoes, pottery and mask making, weaving baskets and carving arrowheads are still carried on, but mostly now for the tourists.

This Eastern Band of Cherokee are descendants of those Cherokee who, in the late 1830s, remained in the mountains of North Carolina rather than be forced to march along the infamous *'Trail of Tears'* to Oklahoma. A large wooden carving of a Cherokee face, sited just outside the Museum in Cherokee, with a large tear running down each cheek, is a poignant and emotive reminder of the hardships and sufferings inflicted on these peoples at the hands of the white man, forced off their lands to seek refuge in alien surroundings, and in an artificial life-style, foreign to their mountain and forest roots. Like the Aborigines of Australia, these peoples are finding it difficult to adjust to their new ways of life, especially as far as their food is concerned. Their bodies are not programmed to eat Western food, especially fast junk food, and they suffer from severe illnesses, especially obesity and diabetes.

These Cherokee Indians who still live here, a branch of the Iroquois nation, can trace their history in this region back over more than one thousand years. Originally, their society was based on hunting, trading and agriculture. They lived in small communities, their homes wooden frames, covered with woven vines and saplings plastered with mud. These were replaced in later years with log structures. To soften their oak beds beneath the buffalo and beaver skins, the women would place feathery boughs of hemlock and broom sage. The Cherokees readily adopted the tools and weapons introduced by Europeans, and desire for these items changed Cherokee life, as they began to hunt animals, not just for food, but also for skins to trade.

Here in their ancient homeland, these North Carolina Cherokee still compete in bowmanship and blow-gun contests, they play the ancient game of Indian Ball and participate in other primitive games and dances that were begun centuries before the white man ventured into the region.

The arrival of the first casino in Cherokee, Harrah's Casino, in 1997, followed soon after by many more, dramatically changed everything from jobs to education and health care for Cherokee tribe members. Manufacturing and textile plants which previously existed in the area have since closed or moved overseas. Before the casino, National Park tourism provided work for about half of the year, and most tribal members lived off public assistance during the Winter. The casino now draws large numbers of people from all over the country to Cherokee, and tourism is now the main source of money for the Cherokee.

These mountains are another world; they exist in a different time zone; they operate on a different, higher vibrational level; the energy is high and strong.

So, what did I find during my time there?

Firstly, the sense of peace and tranquillity; being removed, physically and Spiritually, from the hustle and noise of every-day life as we know it. The feeling of calm and serenity was palpable, tangible, enveloping everything and oozing into everywhere, the noise of traffic conspicuous by its absence. A veil of hushed reverence, a veil of hushed silence hung over everything, enveloping, enfolding, protecting, warding off the harsh fragmentative noises of the outside world; a silence that penetrated into every corner of this forested time warp, a silence that went far beyond just mere quiet; an all-pervading silence that fed into my very soul, nourishing, renewing, replenishing;

84

Spirit Calling - Are You Listening?

an all-enveloping deafening silence that echoed throughout my very being, forcing me to hear the sounds of Nature that reverberated above and beyond the silence itself; the inter-connectedness between all of God's creatures as they conversed and communicated, as they rambled and wandered, glided and soared, perched and nestled. I was forced to just be. To just be, in the here and now. There was nowhere else; there was no other place.

There is a Spirit in the woods. That Spirit was palpable, tangible. It was everywhere; watching through unseen eyes; listening with unseen ears; welcoming. It spoke through the silence; soothing, calming, reassuring, enfolding me in arms of warmth and love. Time meant nothing; my watch, shrunk to a mere non-entity, an illusionary, worldly, meaningless intrusion into this other world, this all-embracing, all-encapsulating reality. I felt my entire being expand outwards and beyond my physical body, filling the great vastness, piercing the great depths, merging with the great Oneness, all my sensory mechanisms heightened, sharpened, raised.

Everything was imbued with a deep consciousness. The manifestation of God, the hand of God, the Spirit of God was everywhere. And the beauty God extols was everywhere.

The Goddess Autumn had arrived on stage, had made her grand entrance, casting her spell over everything. Ravishing, hypnotic, alluring, attired in all her magnificent, glorious, spectacular grandeur; a kaleidoscopic undulating extravaganza of colour and texture; twirling, pirouetting, dancing, swirling, pulsating, throbbing, writhing, quivering in a burning inferno of dark ruby reds, bright crimsons, sparkling emerald greens and jades, deep scarlets, cherry reds, copper golds, rustic browns, mustards, speckled yellows, mottled whites. Demanding full attention from her captive audience, she held the stage in her captivating display, her intoxicating performance, resplendent in her unequalled beauty and feverish magnificence. A superb grand finale, a euphoric, climactic last release, a final encore before retiring to the welcoming arms of Mother Earth for the long winter sojourn, that part of the cycle of life, for replenishing and nourishing in preparation for the grand re-entry at the heralding of spring. Her pure, innocent, uncontaminated essence, pointed irrefutably to the profound glory of God's existence; a greater power that controls the massiveness of creation; a Higher Force with a Grand Design, a Grand Plan; an all-knowing Over-Seer that truly delights in the creation of beauty and truly delights in our appreciation of that wondrous beauty.

Even in the rain, the hand of God, the glory of Creation, Divine infusion, was in evidence. Tiny little water bombs plunged from above, cascading down alongside each other in free fall, in a grand extravaganza of Divinely choreographed twirls, twists and meanderings, to finally explode in an effervescent myriad of pulsating joy. Little sparkling crystal beads that clung to everything, dancing, nourishing, replenishing, holding on for dear life to the ends of the leaves, the branches, the grass. Little tiny jewels, little priceless pearls dropping from Heaven, pouring down in a mantle of mystical, moving vapour, each unique in itself, each bearing testimony to the grandeur and splendour of God, each a vital link in the essence of the Grand Design. A cacophony of sounds reverberated through the trees, each drop of rain on each leaf, on each branch, on each blade of grass creating its own unique note, its own unique tone, its own unique contribution to the melodious harmony of the entire synchronised orchestra.

Why exactly had I come here? What had I hoped to find? What was I seeking? Did I find in these mystical forested mountains that which I sought?

I had hoped to experience a Oneness with all Creation, a Oneness with Spirit, a Oneness with Divine Origins. And I had hoped to

Spirit Calling - Are You Listening?

experience the feeling of infinity, the feeling of timelessness, the feeling of belonging in this vast network of Divine Creation, where a power, a force greater than us, has everything in control, everything in order, everything in Divine hold.

And yes, I did find that which I sought!

In this state of expanded awareness, expanded consciousness, in the midst of the silence, in the midst of the spirits of the forest, in the midst of the grand, exotic, intoxicating beauty surrounding me, watched by the winged, the two-legged and the four-legged, the mists of time parted, revealing a vast infinity, a never-ending expanse where all life is immortal, where all forms of life are connected in the One great universal energy of Divinity. To experience this feeling of infinity, as I did in the forests of these mountains, is to feel surrounded by a vastness, an unending space, an unfathomable depth, where one has had no beginning, where there will be no end; where one's existence will continue in an evolutionary process of a continuous changing of energy form; where we are part of an eternal on-going plan, a plan that will guide us all back home to from whence we came, and where we all belong,- in Divine Source.

And the strong message I received? Acceptance! Everything that happens, happens for a purpose; everything is part of the Divine Grand Design. We cannot see the whole picture with our limited earthly, human vision. But, like the eagle, we must fly above earthly matters, accepting that there is a reason and purpose behind absolutely everything and everyone. We are all woven into the exquisite tapestry, all part of the inter-weaving lines, circles and geometric designs that form the vast network of life, on our planet earth, through all the universes, through the entire cosmos.

And yes, I experienced physical healing!

Native American drumming or vision drumming, works on sound

vibrations. As the drumming around me intensified, the flames from the candles began to dance higher and higher up along the walls. I did not experience any visions; nor did I '*travel*' anywhere, as is usually done during Shamanic drumming sessions. Instead, in just a short period into the session, I suddenly felt a massive surge of energy enter into my crown chakra and proceed down through my other chakras. This energy travelled up and down my entire body several times, and then seemed to concentrate entirely on my legs. My legs and feet became very agitated, uneasy, disturbed, unsettled. I have been suffering from swollen lower legs, ankles and feet for about a year now, probably partly the result of long-haul flights and from being exposed to extreme hot climates. I had been concerned, however, when the swelling continued, and had medical tests done for possible blood clots, heart, kidneys, etc, but no problem was found. As the drumming came to an end, my legs began to return to a normal peaceful state. It was only next morning that I noticed a remarkable reduction in the swelling. And as I write this, three weeks later, the swelling has disappeared. The energy generated from the drumming creates its own vibrational frequencies, and knows where to go for each individual. I was not meant to experience any vision, because obviously that was not what I needed at that particular time. How well the energy knew I needed healing! And how well it was able to administer that healing!

And as an added bonus, on the evening before I was due to leave, I was joined on the verandah, for the very first time, by the elusive white owl. Absent up until now, it announced its arrival through a series of hoots and toots. It observed from a near-by tree and then flew off into the darkness, continuing to hoot back at me. Just confirmation that I was in the right place and that all was well, all was as it should be!

All part of my amazing experiences in the land of the Cherokee!

CHAPTER 12

RETURN TO THE GARDEN

Declan Quigley

In the last few decades of the 20th Century and the beginning of the new millennium, there has been a marked rise in our Spiritual consciousness as a species. There is a wider understanding and acknowledgement of the Spiritual forces and energies that act upon our world and ourselves. As prophesised by many Ancient cultures, such as the Maya, the Hopi and many others, there has been a significant change since 2012.

It hasn't been as dramatic and fear-inducing as Hollywood would have had us believe, but then again, as Eileen has suggested earlier, this rise in consciousness is just a return to an old familiar place and understanding. If the initial loss of this Spiritual connection and resultant Spiritual exile was our fall from the *'Garden of Eden'*, then this new rise in our Spiritual consciousness is our *'Return to the Garden'*.

In terms of how our modern world is changing, there has certainly been a break up of old control structures and a diminishing of the power of undermining political and religious organisations. There is a growing acknowledgement that, what were previously believed to be advancements, such as industrialisation, globalisation and the rise of the multi-nationals, have had an extremely detrimental effect on the human race and the world in which we live.

In the last few years, however, some scientific advances, most notably within quantum physics, are highlighting the benefit of *'ancient technologies'* and the understanding of our ancestors. There is even some suggestion from reputable, peer-reviewed, scientific research, that there may be external intelligent forces in operation in our universe affecting the natural world and us. This can be seen as a huge reconnection of Science and Spirituality.

Max Planck, the father of quantum theory, proposed a universal field of energy, that connects all things in creation: *"All matter originates and exists only by virtue of a force...We must assume behind this force the existence of a conscious and intelligent mind. This mind is the matrix of all matter".* – Max Planck, 1944 (Braden, 2007)

In research carried out by the Institute of HeartMath, when individuals live in the same space for a prolonged period of time, there is a synchronisation of brain wave frequency, heart signatures and menstrual cycles. This suggests a very clear and predictable energetic connection between humans. (Wilcock, 2011)

Since the 1950's, notably in USSR/Russia, a significant body of scientific research has been carried out on what has been called the *'Source Field'.* It is suggested that this Source Field contains all possible information and knowledge and can be connected with, to access this information and also to access forms of healing. (Wilcock, 2011)

This research would also suggest that some of the great scientific leap forwards in our history have come at the same time. The idea here is that once the research information appeared in the *Source Field,* it was immediately accessible to all.

In other words, various unconnected inventors came up with the same idea at roughly the same time. Examples of these synchronicities include the invention of the telephone, the electric battery, radio, the steam engine and many more.

Bradwell, (1928) highlights that in the year of 1928, 148 patents for similar inventions and discoveries were applied for at the same time. (Wilcock. 2011) This would concur with Carl Jung's concept of the *'collective consciousness',* or collective human soul. (Jung, 1936)

In separate research, biologist, Rupert Sheldrake, proposed the idea of Morphic, or *'Morphogenic Fields'*, which are a similar concept as the Source Field. Sheldrake carried out research on monkeys on an island off South America, and found that once one monkey discovered how to carry out a beneficial task, this rapidly spread to the whole population of monkeys on the island.

Further to this, in a very short space of time this new learned behaviour was observed in many areas of South America and then eventually in other continents. It was clear to Sheldrake that because of the geographic spread and the timeline involved, it would have been impossible for this behaviour to have been learned from the original participants in the research. Sheldrake suggests that this is due to a *'common field of consciousness'*. (Darnell, 2003)

Whilst working for the CIA, Cleve Backster, (1966) discovered that by measuring plants with a polygraph, there was a very significant reaction when they were threatened or physically harmed. Further to that, when those researchers carrying out the study, approached separate plants in a separate room, the same reaction was found, even though the plants were not threatened or harmed. This again would suggest that there is a field of intelligence that is being tapped into by these plants. (Wilcock. 2011)

Lynn McTaggert, in her seminal work *'The Field'* (2002), suggests that the universe is unified by an interactive field, which she calls *'Zero Point Field'*. In her later book, *'The Intention Experiment'*, she suggests that the universe is connected by a quantum energy field and can be influenced by thought and our intention.

Kevin Kelly and Steven Johnson, (2010) have highlighted what they call the *'Hyde Model'*, which suggests that bacteria can be sharing the same mind as us. Dysfunctional body conditions can then be influenced by mind, and at a distance, suggesting an external energetic connection. Fundamentally, this would confirm the belief that energetic healing by touch, and even at a distance is not only possible, but has a scientific underpinning. (Kelly and Johnson, 2010)

Anna Wise, (1996) discovered that there are consistent and predictable brainwave patterns amongst those engaged in psychic, shamanic and yogic states. These brainwave frequencies are found amongst those engaged in energetic healing. (Darnell, 2003).

As we can see from this wealth of research, there is a growing understanding that we, as individuals, are much more powerful and fundamentally connected than previously thought. This is the return to the understanding of our old cultures and beliefs.

In recent times, the popularity of ancient Spiritual philosophies, such as shamanism, are promoting individual power, individual responsibility and a direct connection to these intelligent universal forces. These philosophies would suggest that there are technologies that give us access to previously dormant abilities, ultimately, allowing us to change our world, heal each other and create a much more beneficial future for ourselves and for those who are following us.

In shamanic philosophy, the oldest form of Spirituality known to human kind, there is the understanding that all matter and consciousness is energy and this energy is connected in a grand web or field of universal energy. This models all of the previously mentioned research and provides a scientific base to this ancient healing practice.

The majority of ancient shaman, in all world cultures, were animists. In *'Animism'*, there is the fundamental belief that every rock, tree, river and creature has a common energy that is Divine in nature and beneficent in attitude. In other words, everything has a common energy running through it and that energy can be called God, Spirit, Source, or Great Spirit, dependent on the particular culture or belief system.

Spirit Calling - Are You Listening?

This being the case, the shaman would tap into this field of energy, for information, guidance and to access healing for the community. This connection with the Divine could potentially be experienced by every individual. Sandra Ingerman, calls this approach, *'The Path of Direct Revelation'*. (Shamanic Journeying, 2008)

This is in stark contrast to the majority of modern religious beliefs in that, with organised religions, we must go through a mediating person or organisation, completely limiting our personal contact with the Divine and completely down-playing our natural ability to connect with Spirit.

The shaman has always been called the *'walker between worlds'*, our world and the world of Spirit. To do this, the shaman uses a technology that is known as the *'shamanic journey'*, a form of ecstatic trance, to tap into this great web of energy. This trance is induced by the use of rapid drumming, dancing, specialized breathing and in some cases with the use of psychedelic substances, such as psilocybin mushrooms, peyote or ayahuasca.

The shaman 'journeys' to the three worlds of Spirit, the Upperworld, the Middleworld and the Lowerworld, for healing, information and to meet Spirit Guides. Unconnected individuals throughout the world, practising shamanic techniques, have found strikingly similar environments, Guides, symbolism and accurate information during their shamanic journeys. (Madden, 2009)

In opposition to mainstream science and organised religion, we can clearly see that there is very definite substance to the concept of a collective field of intelligence, and the idea that we can heal whilst connected with this intelligence. This may have been what was happening to Eileen, during her drum healing, whilst with the Cherokee .

Eileen describes how she felt the energy enter at the crown chakra, aided by the frequency of the drum. This is a perfect example of the shamanic healing process. In shamanic thought, the drum holds its own energy, an independent healing energy. When used on the body this energy has a very powerful effect and as Eileen explains, this was a profound experience.

Whilst this healing was commencing, the shaman would be connecting to the great web of energy, Source Field or Morphogenic Field, where the helping Spirits would be accessible. The shaman would then seek to align the energies of Spirit with the energies of the person being healed, thus creating a very fundamental and powerful healing.

Certainly, there is a bank of very compelling evidence to suggest that all this and more is possible. It is apparent that there is much more to these concepts than is being acknowledged by mainstream science, religion and medicine. The ancient peoples knew it, wrote about it and passed it down though the generations within their cultures. The question is, why then has this knowledge been disregarded for so long?

One can only surmise that, at certain points throughout our history, it was decided that it would be more prudent to minimise the importance of tapping into this universal field of energy. And not only minimise this, but demonize it! What better way to control the people than to cut them off from their Divine nature, connection to God and natural ability to heal each other?

With a diminishing of the stranglehold of organised religion, the fall of many authoritarian political regimes and mass access to information through the internet, it would appear that we are placed in a position of potential freedom of mind and choice. It is also abundantly clear, that the aforementioned social structures were active in undermining old wisdom and knowledge and technologies.

This situation may be ushering in a new age of enlightenment, or at the very least, we are going full circle and discovering that, far from being mindless barbarians, our ancestors had a much more developed and sophisticated outlook with their societies.

Amongst the Andean shaman, it is acknowledged that this is the time of *'Pachacooti'*, or great healing and advancement of Mother Earth. As we are all aware, the Mayan calendar has prophesised a time of great social change in our world, with the mid-point being 2012. They suggest that after this time, the earth and its people would be completely unrecognisable.

As Victor Hugo said: *'There is nothing more powerful than an idea whose time has come'*. This may now be that very time!

It would appear that a review of our true Spiritual nature is long overdue.

Perhaps it is time to return to the ways of the ancients, or at least incorporate this ancient wisdom into the wisdom and advancements of the 21st Century.

Perhaps it's time to *Return to the Garden!*

Declan Quigley, January 2016.

Declan Quigley of Anam Nasca, is a Spiritual Author, Shamanic Practitioner and Tutor based in County Down, Ireland. He can be contacted on anamnasca@gmail.com

Eileen McCourt

EPILOGUE

OUR ULTIMATE DESTINY?

We are Saints in the making, destined for perfection. Only I don't think the Saints and Angels need get too excited just yet about us joining them! Most of us still have a long, long way to go!

As a species, we are the infants in the whole story of creation. And like infants, we can only progress with baby steps.

We are all seekers.

As seekers, we need to have the courage to step into and embrace the unknown. We need to accept that the nature of life lies in its unpredictability, its transience, its changeability, its impermanence. We must be open to all that life has to offer.

As seekers on our Spiritual path, we need to discard the need for material gain, to go beyond transient, temporary material satisfaction and accept that there are other levels of existence beyond the vibrational level of planet earth and beyond our five human physical senses.

We need to understand that planet earth, its sun, its moon, its constellations of stars are all but a microcosm within the macrocosm of the entire totality of creation. Yet we mortals, in our self-imposed ignorance, still cling fervently to our long-held beliefs, and still identify with linear and spatial boundaries that do not exist.

We are all seeking the truth; the universal truth. We are on a mission to uncover, not to discover, the truth. The truth has always been with us, but it has been hidden, distorted, manipulated by those who would control us for their own ends.

"All great truths begin as blasphemies." So wrote George Bernard Shaw, the late nineteenth, early twentieth century, Oscar-winning Irish playwright and critic.

The truth comes to us all when we are ready to receive it and accept it. The process of receiving the truth is the process of Awakening, the process of Ascension, the process of achieving Enlightenment.

We can only awaken those who who are ready to be awakened; and with each person who awakens, the process of increasing collective consciousness, collective awareness, gathers momentum.

We must be awakened to the awareness that our beliefs create the world in which we live. Our beliefs bring about our actions. And our actions have brought our world to the brink of destruction.

And why? Because our beliefs are NOT the truths.

We believe that the problems in our world today are political and economic problems. But our problems are neither political nor economic.

The problem in our world today is a Spiritual problem. And because the problems are Spiritual problems, then the solution lies obviously in Spirituality.

And why must we look for a Spiritual solution? We must seek a Spiritual solution simply because we are Spiritual beings! That's why!

Once we understand this, once we see the truth and accept it, then we will have the solution. It is what we believe that makes us act in a certain way.

And we can see that we are acting in a way that is not achieving the best results for humanity or for planet earth.

As we exit the Age of Pisces, the age of believing, where we believed everything we were taught, and now enter the Age of Aquarius, which is the age of knowing, we are beginning to uncover the universal truth, to know the universal truth.

We are going through a great awakening process. We are here to re-learn, to re-member who we really are! To find the parts of the jig-saw and put it all together again!

We each have our own jig-saw to re-assemble. Each of us, alone, must bear total responsibility for our own deaf ear, our own blind eye. Each of us, alone, controls our own destiny. Each of us, alone, must find the courage to live according our own spirit's promptings, to read our own spirit's sign-posts.

We cannot live our lives according to the dictates of anyone else. We must have the courage to be different; have the courage to follow our own inner wisdom; have the courage to step outside of the material world with all its inherent, artificial trappings.

And above all else, we must have the courage to question our long-held beliefs, because in questioning such beliefs, we will find the truth. When we find the truth, we will change our beliefs. And when we change our beliefs, we will change our behaviour.

Spirit is calling us! Calling us to find the great universal truth! The great universal truth of who we really are! The great universal truth about the nature of God, the nature of life and why we are all here!

But the question is, are we listening?

Eileen McCourt